AROUND the WORLD in KNITTED

SOCKS

AROUND the WORLD in KNITTED

SOCKS

26 INSPIRED DESIGNS

STEPHANIE VAN DER LINDEN

INTERWEAVE.
interweavestore.com

Editor Anne Merrow
Technical Editor Karen Frisa
Translation C. Elizabeth Wellenstein
Cover & Interior Design nice kern, llc
Photography Frechverlag, except pages 43, 51, 65, 75, and 109 (iStockphoto.com)
Production Design Katherine Jackson

The original German edition was published as *Socken aus aller Welt.*
© 2008 frechverlag GmbH, Stuttgart, Germany (www.web.de)
This edition is published by arrangement with Claudia Böhme Rights
& Literary Agency, Hannover, Germany (www.agency-boehme.com).

First North American edition published in 2010 by Interweave Press LLC.

Interweave Press LLC
201 East Fourth Street
Loveland, CO 80537-5655 USA
interweavestore.com

Printed in China by Asia Pacific Offset Ltd.

Library of Congress Cataloging-in-Publication Data
Linden, Stephanie van der.
[Socken aus aller Welt. English]
Around the world in knitted socks : 26 inspired designs / Stephanie van der Linden.
p. cm.
Includes index.
ISBN 978-1-59668-230-6
1. Knitting--Patterns. 2. Socks. I. Title.
TT825.L54 2010
746.43'2--dc22
2010008140

10 9 8 7 6 5 4 3 2 1

FOREWORD
KNITTING AROUND THE WORLD

In the course of the last century, knitting has reached almost every corner of the world—knit and purl stitches are familiar in almost every culture. Although the basic techniques are the same everywhere, there is always something new to be discovered from local patterns and motifs. Creative elements and special techniques have spread along trade routes and through colonization. They appeared in new places, put down roots, and evolved along with the local textile and ceramic patterns that were common in a given country.

Originally reserved exclusively for men, sock knitting became a job for women as well and was passed down from generation to generation. Socks were valued not only as accessories that protected feet and kept them warm, but also as decorative pieces.

In addition to different patterns, different methods of sock knitting have developed as well. For example, in Europe socks are knitted from cuff to toe, while in Turkey and many Balkan states, socks are knitted from toe to cuff. The inspiration for the patterns in this book was drawn from many different cultures. Discover the diversity of color and design on a journey through the world of sock knitting.

Happy knitting!

STEPHANIE VAN DER LINDEN

CONTENTS

ALPINE GLOW

GERMANY

Heavily cabled patterns made up of twisted and traveling stitches are characteristic of designs of Alpine regions. In this design, the traditional "forgotten love" clock pattern travels diagonally across the instep of the sock.

Finished size 8 (8½, 8¾)" (20.5 [21.5, 22] cm) foot circumference and 10 (10½, 10¾)" (25.5 [26.5, 27.5] cm) long from back of heel to tip of toe. To fit U.S. women's shoe sizes 5–6½ (7–8½, 9–10½) (European sizes 36–37 [38–39, 40–41]). Socks shown measure 10½" (26.5 cm) long.

Yarn Fingering (Super Fine #1). *Shown here:* Regia 4-ply (75% wool, 25% nylon; 229 yd [209 m]/50 g): #2191 terra, 2 balls.

Needles U.S. size 0 (2 mm) for smallest size, or U.S. size 1 (2.25 mm) for 2 larger sizes: set of 5 double-pointed (dpn). Adjust needle size if necessary to obtain the correct gauge.

Notions Markers (m); cable needle (cn); tapestry needle.

Gauge 32 sts and 42 rnds = 4" (10 cm) in St st for smallest size; 30 sts and 42 rnds = 4" (10 cm) in St st for 2 larger sizes.

Notes For U.S. women's shoe sizes 5–6½ (European sizes 36–37), work pattern as given to end of heel. For a shorter foot, work increases and deceases for diagonal traveling pattern every 3rd round (instead of every 4th round).

For U.S. women's shoe sizes 9–10½ (European sizes 40–41), work Row 1 of Diagonal chart as an increase round just as for Rows 5, 9, 13, 17, 21, and 25.

RIGHT SOCK

CUFF

CO 75 sts. Divide sts onto 4 dpn (19 sts each on Needles 1–3, 18 sts on Needle 4), place marker (pm), and join for working in the rnd, being careful not to twist sts.

Work in k2 through back loop (tbl), p1 rib for 12 rnds.

LEG

DIAMOND

Work Rows 1–40 of Leg chart—72 sts rem; 18 sts on each needle.

CLOCK

Begin diagonal patt as foll:

NEXT RND NEEDLE 1 K6, work 12 sts according to Vertical chart; **NEEDLE 2** Pm, work Row 1 of Left Diagonal chart (see Notes), knit to end; **NEEDLES 3 AND 4** Knit—71 (71, 72) sts rem; 18 sts each on Needles 1, 3, and 4, 17 (17, 18) sts on Needle 2.

Work in patt as established, working Vertical and Diagonal charts on Needles 1 and 2 and working in St st on Needles 3 and 4, to end of Vertical chart—diagonal patt has shifted to end of needle.

HEEL

Place first 18 sts of rnd and last 18 sts of rnd onto one needle—36 sts for heel.

Heel will be worked back and forth in rows on these 36 sts; rem 35 (35, 36) sts will be worked later for instep. Cut yarn and, with RS facing, reattach at beg of Needle 4.

HEEL FLAP

Work back and forth in rows for 32 rows, working sts as they appear and ending with a WS row.

TURN HEEL

Work short-rows (see Glossary) as foll:

SHORT-ROW 1 (RS) K19, ssk, k1, turn.

SHORT-ROW 2 Sl 1, p3, p2tog, p1, turn.

SHORT-ROW 3 Sl 1, knit to 1 st before gap created on previous row, ssk, k1, turn.

SHORT-ROW 4 Sl 1, purl to 1 st before gap created on previous row, p2tog, p1, turn.

LEG

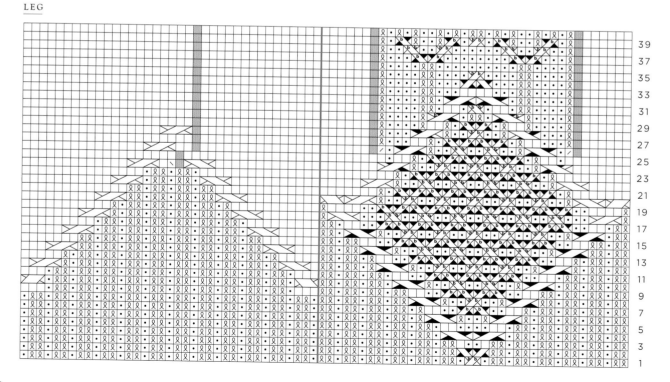

Rep Short-rows 3 and 4 six more times—20 heel sts rem.

SHAPE GUSSET

NEXT RND With an empty needle (Needle 1), k20 heel sts, pick up and knit 16 sts along edge of heel flap; knit to m, work Row 1 of Left Diagonal chart (see Notes), knit to end (Needles 2 and 3); with another needle (Needle 4), pick up and knit 16 sts along edge of heel flap, k10 from Needle 1—86 (86, 88) sts total; 26 sts each on Needles 1 and 4; 17 (17, 18) sts each on Needles 2 and 3. Instep is worked on Needles 2 and 3; sole is worked on Needles 1 and 4.

NEXT RND NEEDLE 1 Knit; **NEEDLES 2 AND 3** Knit to m, work Left Diagonal chart, knit to end; **NEEDLE 4** Knit.

Work 1 more rnd in patt as established.

LEFT DIAGONAL

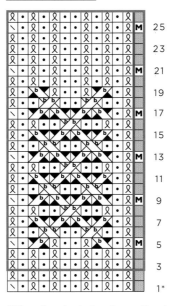

* There is a dec but no inc on Row 1

VERTICAL

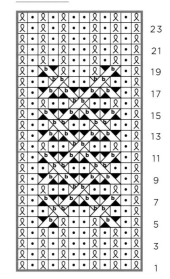

□ knit

• purl

ℓ k1tbl

／ k2tog

＼ ssk

M M1

▨ no stitch

□ pattern repeat

| marker position

| end of Needle 2

sl 1 st onto cn, hold in back, k1, p1 from cn

sl 1 st onto cn, hold in front, p1, k1 from cn

sl 1 st onto cn, hold in back, k1tbl, k1tbl from cn

sl 1 st onto cn, hold in front, k1tbl, k1tbl from cn

sl 1 st onto cn, hold in back, k1tbl, p1 from cn

sl 1 st onto cn, hold in front, p1, k1tbl from cn

sl 1 st onto cn, hold in back, k2, k1 from cn

sl 2 sts onto cn, hold in front, k1, k2 from cn

sl 2 sts onto cn, hold in back, k2, k2 from cn

sl 2 sts onto cn, hold in front, k2, k2 from cn

sl 2 sts onto cn, hold in back, k2, p2 from cn

sl 2 sts onto cn, hold in front, p2, k2 from cn

sl 2 sts onto cn, hold in front, (k1, p1), k2 from cn

sl 2 sts onto cn, hold in back, k2, (p1, k1tbl) from cn

sl 2 sts onto cn, hold in front, (k1tbl, p1), k2 from cn

sl 2 sts onto cn, hold in back, k2, (k1tbl, p1) from cn

sl 2 sts onto cn, hold in front, (p1, k1tbl), k2 from cn

NEXT RND (dec rnd) **NEEDLE 1** Knit to last 3 sts, k2tog, k1; **NEEDLES 2 AND 3** Work in patt as established; **NEEDLE 4** K1, ssk, knit to end—2 sts dec'd.

Rep last 3 rnds 8 more times—68 (68, 70) sts rem; 17 sts each on Needles 1 and 4; 17 (17, 18) sts each on Needles 2 and 3.

FOOT

Work even in patt as established until Diagonal chart reaches end of instep sts (chart Row 4 [21, 21]).

NEXT RND Knit to m, work Row 5 (22, 22) of Vertical chart, knit to end.

Work in patt as established until foot measures 7½ (8, 8¼)" (19 [20.5, 21] cm) from back of heel.

Knit 1 rnd.

NEXT RND **NEEDLE 1** Knit; **NEEDLE 2** K1, [ssk] 0 (0, 1) time, knit to end; **NEEDLE 3** Knit to last 0 (0, 3) sts, [k2tog, k1] 0 (0, 1) time; **NEEDLE 4** Knit—68 sts rem; 17 sts on each needle.

TOE

NEXT RND (dec rnd) **NEEDLES 1 AND 3** Knit to last 3 sts, k2tog, k1; **NEEDLES 2 AND 4** K1, ssk, knit to end—4 sts dec'd.

Rep dec rnd every 4th rnd once more, every 3rd rnd 2 times, every 2nd rnd 3 times, then every rnd 8 times—8 sts rem.

FINISHING

Break yarn, leaving an 8" (20.5 cm) tail. With tail threaded on a tapestry needle, draw through rem sts and pull tight. Fasten off on WS. Weave in loose ends.

RIGHT DIAGONAL

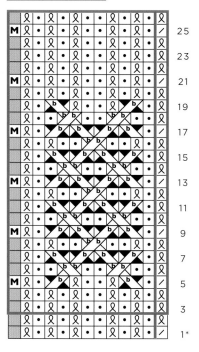

* There is a dec but no inc on Row 1

	knit
	purl
	k1tbl
	k2tog
	ssk
M	M1
	no stitch
	pattern repeat
	marker position
	end of Needle 2

sl 1 st onto cn, hold in back, k1, p1 from cn

sl 1 st onto cn, hold in front, p1, k1 from cn

sl 1 st onto cn, hold in back, k1tbl, k1tbl from cn

sl 1 st onto cn, hold in front, k1tbl, k1tbl from cn

sl 1 st onto cn, hold in back, k1tbl, p1 from cn

sl 1 st onto cn, hold in front, p1, k1tbl from cn

LEFT SOCK

CUFF

CO 75 sts. Divide sts onto 4 dpn (19 sts each on Needles 1–3, 18 sts on Needle 4), place marker (pm), and join for working in the rnd, being careful not to twist sts.

Work in k2 through back loop (tbl), p1 rib for 12 rnds.

LEG

DIAMOND

Work Rows 1–40 of Leg chart—72 sts rem; 18 sts on each needle.

CLOCK

Begin diagonal patt as foll:

NEXT RND NEEDLE 1 K5, work Row 1 of Right Diagonal chart (see Notes), pm as indicated on chart; **NEEDLE 2** Work 12 sts according to Vertical chart (see page 11), k6; **NEEDLES 3 AND 4** Knit—71 (71, 72) sts rem; 17 (17, 18) sts on Needle 1, 18 sts each on Needles 2–4.

Work in patt as established, working Diagonal and Vertical charts on Needles 1 and 2 and working in St st on Needles 3 and 4, to end of Vertical chart—diagonal patt has shifted to beg of needle.

HEEL

Place 18 sts of Needle 2 and 18 sts of Needle 3 onto one needle—36 sts for heel.

Heel will be worked back and forth in rows on these 36 sts; rem 35 (35, 36) sts will be worked later for instep. Cut yarn and, with RS facing, reattach at beg of Needle 2.

HEEL FLAP

Work back and forth in rows for 32 rows, working sts as they appear and ending with a WS row.

TURN HEEL

Work short-rows as foll:

SHORT-ROW 1 (RS) K19, ssk, k1, turn.

SHORT-ROW 2 Sl 1, p3, p2tog, p1, turn.

SHORT-ROW 3 Sl 1, knit to 1 st before gap created on previous row, ssk, k1, turn.

SHORT-ROW 4 Sl 1, purl to 1 st before gap created on previous row, p2tog, p1, turn.

Rep Short-rows 3 and 4 six more times—20 heel sts rem.

SHAPE GUSSET

NEXT RND Arrange and renumber needles as foll: With an empty needle (Needle 1), k20 heel sts, pick up and knit 16 sts along edge of heel flap; knit to 2 sts before m, work Row 1 of Right Diagonal chart (see Notes), knit to end (Needles 2 and 3); with another needle (Needle 4), pick up and knit 16 sts along edge of heel flap, k10 from Needle 1—86 (86, 88) sts total; 26 sts each on Needles 1 and 4; 17 (17, 18) sts each on Needles 2 and 3. Instep is worked on Needles 2 and 3; sole is worked on Needles 1 and 4.

NEXT RND NEEDLE 1 Knit; **NEEDLES 2 AND 3** Knit to chart, work Right Diagonal chart, knit to end; **NEEDLE 4** Knit.

Work 1 more rnd in patt as established.

NEXT RND (dec rnd) **NEEDLE 1** Knit to last 3 sts, k2tog, k1; **NEEDLES 2 AND 3** Work in patt as established; **NEEDLE 4** K1, ssk, knit to end—2 sts dec'd.

Rep last 3 rnds 8 more times—68 (68, 70) sts rem; 17 sts each on Needles 1 and 4; 17 (17, 18) sts each on Needles 2 and 3.

FOOT

Work even in patt as established until Diagonal chart reaches beg of instep sts (chart Row 4 [21, 21]).

NEXT RND Knit to 1 st before m, work Row 5 (22, 22) of Vertical chart, removing m, knit to end.

Work in patt as established until foot measures 7½ (8, 8¼)" (19 [20.5, 21] cm) from back of heel.

Knit 1 rnd.

NEXT RND NEEDLE 1 Knit; **NEEDLE 2** K1, [ssk] 0 (0, 1) time, knit to end; **NEEDLE 3** Knit to last 0 (0, 3) sts, [k2tog, k1] 0 (0, 1) time; **NEEDLE 4** Knit—68 sts rem; 17 sts on each needle.

TOE

Work toe and finish as for right sock.

DELFT BLUE

THE NETHERLANDS

With minimal influence from neighboring countries, Dutch knitting designs have remained very distinctive. Stranded-knitting patterns in strong clear colors reflect inspiration from embroidery and quilting as well as ceramic tiles and stoneware.

Finished size 9¼" (23.5 cm) foot circumference and 10" (25.5 cm) long from back of heel to tip of toe. To fit U.S. women's shoe sizes 8–10½ (European sizes 39–41).

Yarn Fingering (Super Fine #1). *Shown here:* Regia 4-ply (75% wool, 25% nylon; 229 yd [209 m]/50 g): #1988 blue, #1992 natural, #2002 red, and #1994 loden (green), 1 ball each.

Needles U.S. size 1 (2.25 mm): set of 5 double-pointed (dpn), or 2 circular (cir) needles. Adjust needle size if necessary to obtain the correct gauge.

Notions 2 markers (m); waste yarn for provisional CO; tapestry needle.

Gauge 36 sts and 40 rnds = 4" (10 cm) in charted patt.

Note This design lends itself to being worked on 2 circular needles instead of dpn (see Glossary).

HEM

With red and using the provisional method (see Glossary), CO 72 sts. Divide sts evenly onto 4 dpn, place marker (pm), and join for working in the rnd, being careful not to twist sts.

Knit 6 rnds. Purl 1 rnd for turning ridge. Knit 7 rnds.

Join hem as foll: Fold fabric at purl rnd. Removing provisional CO as you go, *pick up first st of CO edge and place it onto left needle; k2tog (picked-up st with next st on needle); rep from * around—72 sts.

LEG

RND 1 *K6, M1 (see Glossary); rep from * to end—84 sts. Work Rows 1–14 of Tile chart once, then work Rows 1–5 once more. Break yarns.

HEEL

Place first 21 sts of rnd and last 22 sts of rnd onto one needle—43 sts total. Heel will be worked back and forth in rows on these 43 sts; rem 41 sts will be worked later for instep.

HEEL FLAP

With RS facing, join natural. Work Rows 1–6 of Heel Heart chart.

NEXT ROW Work 1 st in St st in natural, work Row 1 of Lozenge chart to last st, work 1 st in St st in natural. Cont in patt, work Rows 1–17 of Lozenge chart 2 times, then work Row 1 once more.

TURN HEEL

With natural, work short-rows (see Glossary) as foll:

SHORT-ROW 1 (RS) K22, ssk, k1, turn.

SHORT-ROW 2 Sl 1, p2, p2tog, p1, turn.

SHORT-ROW 3 Sl 1, knit to 1 st before gap created on previous row, ssk, k1, turn.

SHORT-ROW 4 Sl 1, purl to 1 st before gap created on previous row, p2tog, p1, turn.

Rep Short-rows 3 and 4 eight more times—23 heel sts rem.

TILE

HEEL HEART

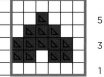

LOZENGE

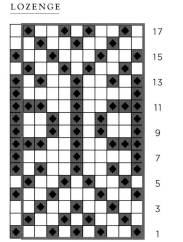

blue

natural

red

green

pattern repeat

SHAPE GUSSET

NEXT RND With natural and an empty needle (Needle 1), k23 heel sts, pick up and knit 20 sts along edge of heel flap; work Row 6 of Tile chart, break blue (Needles 2 and 3); with natural and another needle (Needle 4), pick up and knit 20 sts along edge of heel flap, k12 from Needle 1—104 sts total; 31 sts on Needle 1, 21 sts on Needle 2, 20 sts on Needle 3, and 32 sts on Needle 4. Beg of rnd is at center of heel.

NEXT RND (dec rnd) **NEEDLE 1** Work 8 sts according to Sole chart, k2tog with blue, pm, work 21 sts according to Row 7 of Tile chart; **NEEDLES 2 AND 3** Work Row 7 of Tile chart; **NEEDLE 4** Work 22 sts according to Row 7 of Tile chart, pm, ssk with blue, beg with st 2 of chart, work 8 sts according to Sole chart—102 sts rem.

NEXT RND **NEEDLE 1** Work Sole chart to 1 st before m, k1 with blue, sl m, work next rnd of Tile chart to end; **NEEDLES 2 AND 3** Work Tile chart; **NEEDLE 4** Work Tile chart to m, sl m, k1 with blue, work Sole chart to end. Work 2 rnds even in patt as established.

NEXT RND (dec rnd) **NEEDLE 1** Work Sole chart to 2 sts before m, k2tog with blue, sl m, work Tile chart; **NEEDLES 2 AND 3** Work Tile chart; **NEEDLE 4** Work Tile chart to m, sl m, ssk with blue, work Sole chart to end—2 sts dec'd.

Rep last 3 rnds 7 more times—86 sts rem.

NEXT RND K2tog with natural (removing m), work in patt to last 2 sts, ssk with blue (removing m)—84 sts rem; Row 5 of Tile chart is complete.

Rearrange sts so that there are 21 sts on each needle.

FOOT

Working sts in rep box only, work Rows 1–17 of Lozenge chart once, then work Rows 1–6 once more and *at the same time* on the first rnd, dec 4 sts evenly spaced around—80 sts rem. Work Rows 1–6 of Foot Heart chart and *at the same time* dec 2 sts evenly spaced on Rows 2 and 6—76 sts rem.

TOE

Change to natural.

NEXT RND (dec rnd) **NEEDLES 1 AND 3** Knit to last 3 sts, k2tog, k1; **NEEDLES 2 AND 4** K1, ssk, knit to end—4 sts dec'd.

Rep dec rnd every 3rd rnd 3 more times, every 2nd rnd 4 times, then every rnd 9 times—8 sts rem.

FINISHING

Break yarn, leaving an 8" (20.5 cm) tail. With tail threaded on a tapestry needle, draw through rem sts and pull tight. Fasten off on WS. Weave in loose ends.

☒	blue
☐	natural
■	red
◆	green
☐	pattern repeat

SOLE

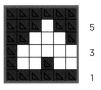

FOOT HEART

FRESH BREEZE

DENMARK

By the fifteenth century, handknitted jackets and stockings were a part of almost every traditional Danish costume. Typical Danish designs feature a large field of patterning interspersed with a small repeating motif and edged with a narrow border.

Finished size 8½" (21.5 cm) circumference and 9¼ (10, 10¼)" (23.5 [25.5, 26] cm) long from back of heel to tip of toe. To fit U.S. women's shoe sizes 5–6½ (7–8½, 9–10½) (European sizes 36–37 [38–39, 40–41]). Socks shown measure 10" (25.5 cm) long.

Yarn Fingering (Super Fine #1). *Shown here:* Regia Silk 4-ply (55% wool, 25% nylon, 20% silk; 219 yd [200 m]/ 50 g): #0054 smoky heather, 2 balls; #0052 gray-blue heather, #0002 natural heather, #0030 fire, and #0091 medium gray heather, 1 ball each.

Needles U.S. size 1 (2.25 mm): set of 5 double-pointed (dpn). Adjust needle size if necessary to obtain the correct gauge.

Notions Marker (m); tapestry needle.

Gauge 34 sts and 38 rnds = 4" (10 cm) in lice patt.

CUFF

With smoky heather, CO 72 sts. Arrange sts evenly onto 4 dpn, place marker (pm), and join for working in the rnd, being careful not to twist sts.

Work in k1 through back loop (tbl), p1 rib for 20 rnds.

LEG

Work Rows 1–14 of Zigzag Border chart.

With gray-blue heather, purl 1 rnd.

Work Rows 1–8 of Wave Border chart.

Work Rows 1–18 of Lice chart, then work Rows 1–11 once more. *Note:* Do not break strand not in use; catch the strand and twist it with the working yarn every 3–5 rnds to secure it as you knit.

HEEL

Heel is worked back and forth using short-rows (see Glossary) over 36 sts of Needles 1 and 4; rem 36 sts will be worked later for instep. Work heel in smoky heather; break other colors.

HEEL TOP

SHORT-ROW 1 (RS) K18, turn.

SHORT-ROW 2 Slyo (see Glossary), p35, turn.

SHORT-ROW 3 Slyo, knit to slyo created on previous row, turn.

SHORT-ROW 4 Slyo, purl to slyo created on previous row, turn.

Rep Short-rows 3 and 4 eleven more times, then work Short-row 3 once more

but do not turn—13 slyo sts at each end of heel, 10 plain sts in center.

Work to end of rnd in St st, being careful to work each slyo as one st. Work 1 more rnd even.

HEEL BOTTOM

Work back and forth on 36 sts of Needles 1 and 4 as foll:

SHORT-ROW 1 (RS) K6, turn.

SHORT-ROW 2 Slyo, p11, turn.

SHORT-ROW 3 Slyo, knit to slyo created on previous row, knit slyo as 1 st, k1, turn.

SHORT-ROW 4 Slyo, purl to slyo created on previous row, purl slyo as 1 st, p1, turn.

Rep Short-rows 3 and 4 eleven more times.

ZIGZAG BORDER

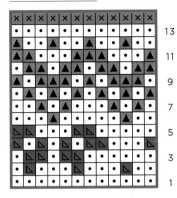

WAVE BORDER

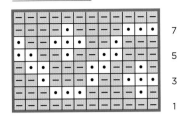

LICE

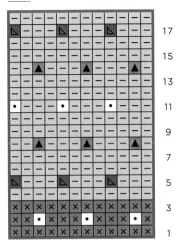

- — smoky heather
- × gray-blue heather
- · natural heather
- ◣ fire
- ▲ medium gray heather
- ☐ pattern repeat

NEXT ROW Slyo, k17 (to end of rnd)—first and last sts of heel are slyos.

FOOT

Resume working in the rnd, working rem 2 slyo as 1 st on first rnd. Work Rows 14–18 of Lice chart, then work Rows 1–18 once, then work Rows 1–16 (1–18, 1–18) once, then work Rows 0 (1–4, 1–8) zero (one, one) time—39 (45, 49) rnds of Lice chart.

TOE

Change to smoky heather.

NEXT RND (dec rnd) **NEEDLES 1 AND 3** Knit to last 3 sts, k2tog, k1; **NEEDLES 2 AND 4** K1, ssk, knit to end—4 sts dec'd.

Rep dec rnd every 3rd rnd 3 more times, every 2nd rnd 4 times, then every rnd 4 times—24 sts rem.

NEXT RND **NEEDLES 1 AND 3** K4, k2tog; **NEEDLES 2 AND 4** Ssk, k4—20 sts rem.

Knit sts on Needle 1. Sl sts from Needle 4 onto Needle 1 and from Needle 3 onto Needle 2. Cut yarn, leaving a 24" (61 cm) tail. With tail threaded on a tapestry needle, use the Kitchener st (see Glossary) to graft rem sts tog. Weave in loose ends.

BY THE FJORDS

NORWAY

ypical Norwegian patterns are worked in stranded two-color knitting, traditionally in black, dark gray, blue, and red with white. The classic Norwegian Star appears in a number of variations, often combined with small symmetrical borders or stripes of patterning.

Finished size 9" (23 cm) foot circumference and 10¼" (26 cm) long from back of heel to tip of toe. To fit U.S. women's shoe sizes 7–9½ (European sizes 38–40).

Yarn Fingering (Super Fine #1). *Shown here*: Regia 4-ply (75% wool, 25% nylon; 229 yd [209 m]/50 g): #1992 natural, #2137 denim, and #2002 cherry red, 1 ball each.

Needles U.S. size 1 (2.25 mm): set of 5 double-pointed (dpn). Adjust needle size if necessary to obtain the correct gauge.

Notions 3 markers (m); tapestry needle.

Gauge 36 sts and 40 rnds = 4" (10 cm) in charted patt.

Note Due to the large pattern repeat, consider working this sock on 2 circular (cir) needles instead of double–pointed needles.

The top of the Instep chart looks like a checkerboard but will work into vertical lines when knitted.

LEG

With denim, CO 80 sts. Arrange sts evenly onto 4 dpn, place marker (pm), and join for working in the rnd, being careful not to twist sts.

Knit 10 rnds for rolled edge.

Work in k1 through back loop (tbl), p1 rib for 10 rnds.

Work Rows 1–40 of Leg chart.

HEEL

Break yarns. Sl first st of Needle 4 to Needle 3. Sl rem 19 sts of Needle 4 to Needle 1, keeping beg of rnd marker in place. Heel will be worked back and forth over 39 sts on Needle 1.

HEEL TOP

With RS facing, reattach denim to first heel st and work short-rows (see Glossary) to shape heel as foll:

SHORT-ROW 1 (RS) K39, turn.

SHORT-ROW 2 Slyo (see Glossary), p38, turn.

SHORT-ROW 3 Slyo, knit to slyo created on previous row, turn.

SHORT-ROW 4 Slyo, purl to slyo created on previous row, turn.

Rep Short-rows 3 and 4 eleven more times, then work Short-row 3 once more but do not turn—13 slyo sts at each end of heel, 13 plain sts in center.

Resume working in the rnd and work to end of rnd, being careful to knit slyo as 1 st, as foll: **NEEDLE 1** Knit with denim; **NEEDLES 2 AND 3** Join natural, work Instep

LEG

39
37
35
33
31
29
27
25
23
21
19
17
15
13
11
9
7
5
3
1

☐ natural

■ denim

✚ cherry red

⟋ k2tog with natural

⟍ ssk with natural

⋋ sl 1, k2tog, psso with natural

☐ pattern repeat

chart, break natural; **NEEDLE 4** Knit with denim. Work 1 more rnd even, attaching natural at beg of Needle 2 and breaking at end of Needle 3.

HEEL BOTTOM

Resume working short-rows on 39 sts of Needles 1 and 4 only as foll:

SHORT-ROW 1 (RS) Knit to last 12 heel sts, turn.

SHORT-ROW 2 Slyo, p14, turn.

SHORT-ROW 3 Slyo, knit to slyo created on previous row, knit slyo as 1 st, k1, turn.

SHORT-ROW 4 Slyo, purl to slyo created on previous row, purl slyo as 1 st, p1, turn.

Rep Short-rows 3 and 4 eleven more times.

NEXT ROW Slyo, knit to beg of rnd, remove m, with another needle (Needle 1), knit to slyo created on previous row, knit slyo as 1 st, pm for new beg of rnd—beg of rnd is now at beg of Needle 2.

FOOT

Resume working in the rnd as foll, working rem slyo as 1 st: **NEEDLES 2 AND 3** Work Instep chart (beg with Row 3); **NEEDLES 4 AND 1** Work Sole chart (beg with Row 1).

Work 30 more rnds in patt as established, ending with Row 33 of Instep chart. *Note:* On Row 20 of Instep chart, substitute cherry red for natural on Sole chart.

NEXT RND **NEEDLES 2 AND 3** Work Row 34 of Instep chart; **NEEDLES 4 AND 1** Work 17 sts of Sole chart, M1 with natural, pm, work 5 sts of Sole chart, pm, M1 with natural, work 16 sts of Sole chart, sl last st of Needle 1 onto Needle 2, and sl first st of Needle 4 onto Needle 3—82 sts; 20 sts on Needle 1, 21 sts on Needle 2, 22 sts on Needle 3, and 19 sts on Needle 4.

MID-FOOT

NEXT RND **NEEDLES 2 AND 3** Work Instep chart to end of Needle 3, work 1 st from Needle 4 onto Needle 3, working it in color as it appears; **NEEDLES 4 AND 1** Knit each st in color as it appears to m, sl m, M1 with color opposite next st on needle, knit each st in color as it appears to next m, M1 with color opposite st just worked, sl m, knit each st in color as it appears to last st of Needle 1, sl last st onto Needle 2—43 sts on Needles 2 and 3, 39 sts on Needles 4 and 1; beg of rnd shifts 1 st to the right.

Rep last rnd through Row 55 of Instep chart, maintaining vertical stripes.

TOE

DEC RND **NEEDLE 2** K1 with natural, ssk with denim, work in vertical stripe patt to end; **NEEDLE 3** Work in vertical stripe patt to last 3 sts, k2tog with denim, k1 with natural; **NEEDLE 4** K1 with denim, ssk with natural, work in vertical stripe patt to end; **NEEDLE 1** Work in vertical stripe patt to last 3 sts, k2tog with natural, k1 with denim—4 sts dec'd.

Rep dec rnd every 4th rnd once more, every 3rd rnd 2 times, every 2nd rnd 3 times, then every rnd 5 times—34 sts rem. Sl 2 sts from Needle 3 onto Needle 4—8 sts each on Needles 1 and 3, 9 sts each on Needles 2 and 4. With denim only, rep dec rnd once more—30 sts rem.

Sl sts from Needle 3 to Needle 2. Sl sts from Needle 4 to Needle 1. Cut yarn, leaving an 8" (20.5 cm) tail. Use Kitchener st (see Glossary) to graft live sts tog. Weave in loose ends.

INSTEP

55
53
51
49
47
45
43
41
39
37
35
33
31
29
27
25
23
21
19
17
15
13
11
9
7
5
3
1

SOLE

1

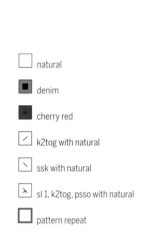

☐ natural

■ denim

✚ cherry red

╱ k2tog with natural

╲ ssk with natural

⅄ sl 1, k2tog, psso with natural

☐ pattern repeat

TRADITIONAL STITCH MOTIFS

ESTONIA

Estonian socks are often knitted with elaborate, colorful stranded-knitting patterns. Imaginative borders are combined with richly decorated tile or lozenge motifs. The braid that frames the cuff is characteristic of Baltic knitting patterns.

Finished size 8¾" (22 cm) foot circumference and 9 (9½, 10¼)" (23 [24, 26] cm) from back of heel to tip of toe. To fit U.S. women's shoe sizes 5–6½ (7–8½, 9–10½) (European sizes 36–37 [38–39, 40–41]). Socks shown measure 9½" (24 cm) long.

Yarn Fingering (Super Fine #1). *Shown here:* Regia 4-ply (75% wool, 25% nylon; 229 yd [209 m]/50 g):

#2199 gray and #1094 pine, 2 balls each, and #0324 marine, 1 ball.

Needles U.S. size 1 (2.25 mm): set of 5 double-pointed (dpn). Adjust needle size if necessary to obtain the correct gauge.

Notions Marker (m); tapestry needle.

Gauge 36 sts and 40 rnds = 4" (10 cm) in charted patt.

CUFF

With marine, CO 84 sts onto 1 dpn. Do not join.

ROW 1 (WS) Knit.

ROW 2 (RS) *K1 with marine, k1 with gray; rep from * and *at the same time* distribute sts evenly onto 4 dpn. Place marker (pm) and join for working in the rnd, being careful not to twist sts.

BRAID

Beg braid with both strands in front of work (see Glossary). Alternate strands as foll: take color to be knit to back of work, knit st, bring to front again.

RND 1 *K1 with marine, k1 with gray, always bringing the new yarn over the one just used; rep from *.

RND 2 *K1 with marine, k1 with gray, always bringing the new yarn under the one just used; rep from *.

RND 3 *K1 with marine, k1 with gray, always bringing the new yarn over the one just used; rep from *.

CUFF PATTERN

RNDS 4–7 Knit with marine.

RND 8 *K1 with marine, k1 with gray; rep from *.

RNDS 9–21 Work Cuff chart.

RND 22 *K1 with marine, k1 with gray; rep from *.

RNDS 23–26 Knit with marine.

RND 27 *K2tog, k19; rep from *—80 sts rem.

LEG

Work Rows 1–24 of Leg chart once, then work Rows 1–12 once more. Break gray.

+ gray

■ marine

= pine

╱ k2tog with pine

╲ ssk with pine

□ pattern repeat

LEG

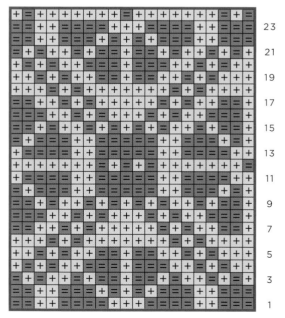

CUFF

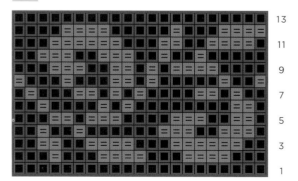

HEEL

HEEL FLAP

With pine, knit to end of Needle 1. Sl sts from Needle 4 to Needle 1, keeping beg of rnd marker in place—40 sts for heel. Heel is worked back and forth on these 40 sts with pine.

DEC ROW (WS) K3, p1, *p2tog, p6; rep from * 3 more times, p1, k3—36 heel sts rem.

NEXT ROW Work 3 sts in garter st, work 30 sts in St st, work 3 sts in garter st.

Cont in patt for 33 more rows, ending with a WS row.

TURN HEEL

Work short-rows (see Glossary) to shape heel as foll:

SHORT-ROW 1 (RS) K19, ssk, k1, turn.

SHORT-ROW 2 Sl 1, p3, p2tog, p1, turn.

SHORT-ROW 3 Sl 1, knit to 1 st before gap created on previous row, ssk, k1, turn.

SHORT-ROW 4 Sl 1, purl to 1 st before gap created on previous row, p2tog, p1, turn.

Rep Short-rows 3 and 4 six more times—20 heel sts rem.

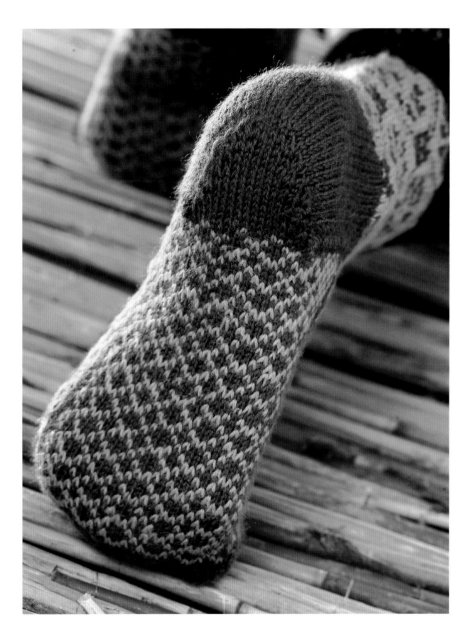

SHAPE GUSSETS

Resume working in the rnd.

NEXT RND (gusset set-up rnd) **NEEDLE 1** K20 heel sts, pick up and knit 17 sts along edge of heel flap; **NEEDLES 2 AND 3** Attach gray and work Row 13 of Leg chart to end of Needle 3, M1 (see Glossary) with gray, break gray; **NEEDLE 4** Pick up and knit 17 sts along other edge of heel flap, k10 from Needle 1—95 sts; 27 sts each on Needles 1 and 4, 20 sts on Needle 2, 21 sts on Needle 3. Break pine and reattach gray and pine at beg of Needle 4. Rnd begins between Needles 3 and 4.

GUSSET RND 1 NEEDLES 4 AND 1 Work Gusset chart; **NEEDLES 2 AND 3** Work Leg chart (see page 32), working last st of Needle 3 as first st of chart.

Cont in patt as established to end of Gusset chart, ending with Row 7 of Leg chart—79 sts rem; 19 sts each on Needles 1 and 4, 20 sts on Needle 2, 21 sts on Needle 3.

FOOT

NEEDLES 4 AND 1 Work Sole chart;
NEEDLES 2 AND 3 Work Leg chart, working last st of Needle 3 as first st of chart. Work even in patt as established for 28 (34, 40) more rnds, ending with Row 12 (18, 24) of Leg chart.

TOE

Break gray and work toe with pine. Knit 1 rnd.

NEXT RND (dec rnd) **NEEDLE 4** *K4, k2tog; rep from * 2 more times, k1; **NEEDLE 1** *K4, k2tog; rep from * 2 more times, k1; **NEEDLE 2** *K3, k2tog; rep from * 3 more times; **NEEDLE 3** *K3, k2tog; rep from * 2 more times, [k1, k2tog] 2 times—64 sts rem; 16 sts on each needle.

TOE DEC RND **NEEDLES 4 AND 2** K1, ssk, knit to end; **NEEDLES 1 AND 3** Knit to last 3 sts, k2tog, k1—4 sts dec'd.

Rep dec rnd every 4th rnd once more, every 3rd rnd 2 times, every 2nd rnd 3 times, then every rnd 7 times—8 sts rem. Break yarn, leaving an 8" (20.5 cm) tail. Thread tail through rem sts, pull tight, and fasten off on WS. Weave in loose ends.

GUSSET

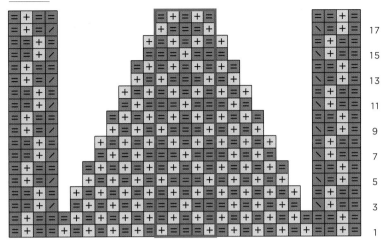

SOLE

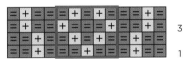

+ gray

■ marine

= pine

∕ k2tog with pine

∖ ssk with pine

☐ pattern repeat

COLORFUL FOLKLORE

LATVIA

The Baltic States are well-known for elaborate and richly detailed mitten designs in which Scandinavian and Russian influences are found. Latvian designs are predominantly black or navy with white and sometimes a bright contrast color.

Finished size 8¾" (22 cm) circumference and 9 (10, 10¾)" (23 [25.5, 27.5] cm) long from back of heel to tip of toe. To fit U.S. women's shoe sizes 5–6½ (7–8½, 9–10½) (European sizes 36–37 [38–39, 40–41]). Socks shown measure 10" (25.5 cm) long.

Yarn Fingering (Super Fine #1). *Shown here:* Regia 4-ply (75% wool, 25% nylon; 229 yd [209 m]/50 g): #0522 charcoal, #1992 natural, and #2002 cherry, 1 ball each.

Needles U.S. size 1 (2.25 mm): set of 5 double-pointed (dpn). Adjust needle size if necessary to obtain the correct gauge.

Notions Marker (m); tapestry needle.

Gauge 36 sts and 40 rnds = 4" (10 cm) in charted patt.

Note The large pattern repeat makes this pattern easy to work on 2 circular needles instead of double-pointed needles.

CUFF

With charcoal, CO 76 sts. Arrange sts evenly onto 4 dpn, place marker (pm), and join for working in the rnd, being careful not to twist sts.

RNDS 1–4 *K1, p1; rep from *.

RND 5 *K1 with charcoal, k1 with cherry; rep from *.

RND 6 Knit with charcoal.

RND 7 *K1 with natural, k3 with charcoal; rep from *.

RND 8 *K1 with natural, [p1, k1, p1] with charcoal; rep from *.

RND 9 *K1 with natural, p1 with charcoal; rep from *.

RNDS 10 AND 12 Rep Rnd 8.

RNDS 11 AND 13 Rep Rnd 9.

RND 14 *K1 with natural, k1 with charcoal; rep from *.

BRAID

Beg braid with both strands in front of work (see Glossary). Alternate strands as foll: take color to be knit to back of work, knit st, bring to front again.

RND 15 *K1 with natural, k1 with charcoal, always bringing the new yarn over the one just used; rep from *.

RND 16 *K1 with natural, k1 with charcoal, always bringing the new yarn under the one just used; rep from *.

RND 17 *K1 with natural, k1 with cherry, always bringing the new yarn over the one just used; rep from *.

RND 18 Knit with natural.

RND 19 (inc rnd; work with natural) **NEEDLES 1 AND 3** Knit to end; **NEEDLES 2 AND 4** M1 (see Glossary), knit to end—78 sts; 19 sts each on Needles 1 and 3, 20 sts each on Needles 2 and 4. Rearrange sts evenly onto 3 dpn (26 sts on each needle).

LEG

Work Rows 1–23 of Leg chart once, then work Rows 1–12 once more.

Break all strands.

HEEL

HEEL FLAP

Sl first 19 sts of rnd and last 20 sts of rnd onto one needle, keeping beg of rnd marker in place—39 sts for heel. Heel is worked back and forth on these 39 sts with charcoal. With RS facing, reattach charcoal. Work 2 transition rows as foll:

ROW 1 (RS; dec row) K8, *k2tog, k8; rep from * once more, k2tog, k9—36 heel sts rem.

ROW 2 (WS) K1, p34, k1.

NEXT ROW (RS) K1, *sl 1 pwise with yarn in back (wyb), k1; rep from * to last st, k1.

NEXT ROW K1, purl to last st, k1.

Rep last 2 rows 16 more times.

LEG

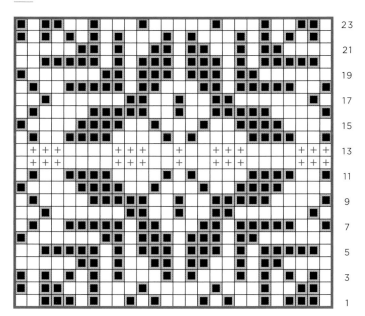

23
21
19
17
15
13
11
9
7
5
3
1

■ charcoal

◪ k2tog with charcoal

◪ ssk with charcoal

□ natural

+ cherry

◹ k2tog with cherry

◲ ssk with cherry

▢ pattern repeat

TURN HEEL

Work short-rows (see Glossary) to shape heel as foll:

SHORT-ROW 1 (RS) K19, ssk, k1, turn.

SHORT-ROW 2 Sl 1, p3, p2tog, p1, turn.

SHORT-ROW 3 Sl 1, knit to 1 st before gap created on previous row, ssk, k1, turn.

SHORT-ROW 4 Sl 1, purl to 1 st before gap created on previous row, p2tog, p1, turn.

Rep Short-rows 3 and 4 six more times—20 heel sts rem.

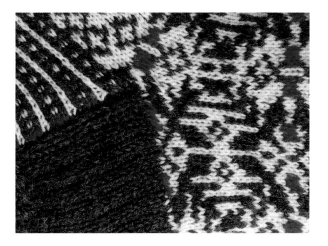

SHAPE GUSSETS

GUSSET SET-UP RND Arrange and work sts as foll: **NEEDLE 1** With charcoal, k20, pick up and knit 17 sts along edge of heel flap; **NEEDLES 2 AND 3** Work 39 sts according to Instep chart; **NEEDLE 4** With charcoal, pick up and knit 17 sts along other edge of heel flap, k10 from Needle 1, M1—94 sts; 27 sts on Needle 1, 39 sts on Needles 2 and 3, 28 sts on Needle 4. Break charcoal and reattach at beg of Needle 4. **NEEDLES 4 AND 1** Work Row 1 of Gusset chart. Beg of rnd is at beg of Needle 2.

NEXT RND NEEDLES 2 AND 3 Work Instep chart; **NEEDLES 4 AND 1** Work Gusset chart.

Cont in patt as established to end of Gusset chart, ending with Row 23 of Instep chart—78 sts rem.

FOOT

NEEDLES 2 AND 3 Work Instep chart; **NEEDLES 4 AND 1** Work Sole chart.

Cont in patt as established for 24 (34, 38) more rnds, ending with Row 2 (12, 16) of Instep chart. Change to charcoal. Knit 1 (1, 4) rnd(s).

TOE

SET-UP RND (dec rnd) **NEEDLE 2** *K3, k2tog; rep from *; **NEEDLE 3** *K3, k2tog; rep from * 2 more times, k4; **NEEDLE 4** *K3, k2tog; rep from *; **NEEDLE 1** *K3, k2tog; rep from * 2 more times, k4—64 sts rem; 16 sts on each needle.

DEC RND NEEDLES 2 AND 4 K1, ssk, knit to end; **NEEDLES 1 AND 3** Knit to last 3 sts, k2tog, k1—4 sts dec'd.

Rep dec rnd every 4th rnd once more, every 3rd rnd 2 times, every other rnd 3 times, then every rnd 7 times—8 sts rem. Break yarn, leaving an 8" (20.5 cm) tail. Thread tail onto tapestry needle, draw through rem sts, pull tight, and fasten off on WS. Weave in loose ends.

SOLE

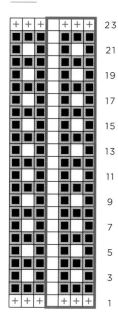

GUSSET

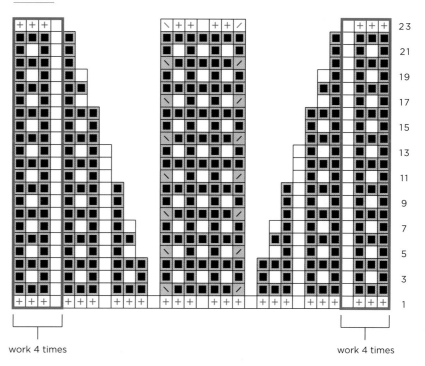

work 4 times

work 4 times

INSTEP

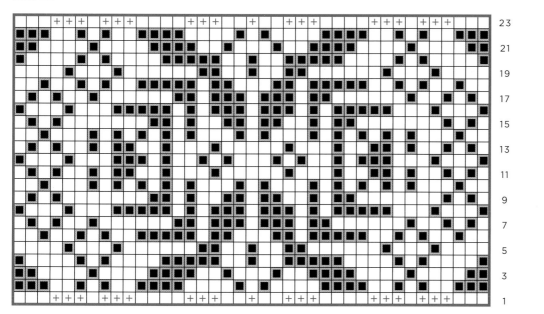

■ charcoal

⁄ k2tog with charcoal

◣ ssk with charcoal

☐ natural

+ cherry

⁄ k2tog with cherry

\ ssk with cherry

☐ pattern repeat

NORDIC INSPIRATION

SWEDEN

Swedish stranded-knitting patterns are often more elaborate and intricately detailed than Norwegian patterns and often use red and white. The patterns may include motifs with pairs of birds combined with hearts, as here, or a ring of dancing people.

Finished size 7¾ (8¼, 8¼)" (19.5 [21, 21] cm) circumference and 9¾ (10¼, 10½)" (25 [26, 26.5] cm) long from back of heel to tip of toe. To fit U.S. women's shoe sizes 5–6½ (7–8½, 9–10½) (European sizes 36–37 [38–39, 40–41]). Socks shown measure 10¼" (26 cm) long.

Yarn Fingering (Super Fine #1). *Shown here:* Regia 4-ply (75% wool, 25% nylon; 229 yd [209 m]/50 g): #1081 ruby and #1992 natural, 1 ball each.

Needles U.S. size 0 (2 mm) for smallest size, or U.S. size 1 (2.25 mm) for 2 larger sizes: set of 5 double-pointed (dpn). Adjust needle size if necessary to obtain the correct gauge.

Notions Marker (m); waste yarn for provisional CO; tapestry needle.

Gauge 36 sts and 42 rnds = 4" (10 cm) in charted patt for smallest size; 34 sts and 40 rnds = 4" (10 cm) in charted patt for larger 2 sizes.

Note This sock is knitted from a provisional cast-on at the toe to the cuff, then stitches are worked from the cast-on to the end of the toe.

PROVISIONAL CAST-ON

With ruby and using the crochet provisional method (see Glossary), CO 70 sts. Divide sts onto 4 dpn (18 sts on Needles 1 and 3, 17 sts on Needles 2 and 4). Place marker (pm) and join for working in the rnd, being careful not to twist sts.

NEXT RND (set-up rnd) Knit 1 rnd, then knit 18 sts of Needle 1. Rnd begins at beg of Needle 2.

FOOT

RNDS 1–50 NEEDLES 2 AND 3 Work Rows 1–50 of Instep chart; **NEEDLES 4 AND 1** Work Rows 1–10 of Sole chart 5 times.

HEEL

With ruby, knit 1 (1, 5) rnd(s). Place last 35 sts of rnd onto one needle. Heel will be worked back and forth in short-rows (see Glossary) over these 35 sts.

HEEL BASE

SHORT-ROW 1 (WS) Slyo (see Glossary), p34, turn.

SHORT-ROW 2 Slyo, knit to slyo created on previous row, turn.

SHORT-ROW 3 Slyo, purl to slyo created on previous row, turn.

Rep Short-rows 2 and 3 ten more times, then work Short-row 2 once more but do not turn—12 slyo sts at each end of heel, 11 plain sts in center.

Knit to end of rnd, then knit 1 more rnd, working each slyo as 1 st. Knit to beg of heel sts.

HEEL BACK

Work back and forth on heel sts as foll:

SHORT-ROW 1 (RS) K24, turn.

SHORT-ROW 2 (WS) Slyo, p12, turn.

SHORT-ROW 3 Slyo, knit to slyo created on previous row, knit slyo as 1 st, k1, turn.

SHORT-ROW 4 Slyo, purl to slyo created on previous row, purl slyo as 1 st, p1, turn.

Rep Short-rows 3 and 4 ten more times.

NEXT ROW Slyo, knit to slyo created on previous row, knit slyo as 1 st.

Divide heel sts onto 2 needles (Needle 4 and Needle 1).

LEG

Resume working in the rnd, working rem slyo as 1 st on first rnd. With ruby, knit 4 rnds.

NEXT RND NEEDLES 2 AND 3 Knit. Rnd begins at beg of Needle 4.

Work Rows 1–10 of Sole chart over all sts 2 times, omitting last 5 sts of chart.

PICOT CUFF

With ruby, knit 7 rnds.

NEXT RND (turning rnd) *K2tog, yo; rep from *.

Knit 6 rnds.

BO all sts loosely. Break ruby, leaving a 30" (76 cm) tail. Fold BO edge to WS at turning rnd. With tail threaded on a tapestry needle, whipstitch hem down.

TOE

Removing provisional CO, place revealed sts onto 4 dpn—70 sts; 18 sts on Needles 1 and 3, 17 sts on Needles 2 and 4.

With ruby, work toe as foll:

DEC RND NEEDLES 1 AND 3 Knit to last 3 sts, k2tog, k1; **NEEDLES 2 AND 4** K1, ssk, knit to end—4 sts dec'd.

Rep dec rnd every 4th rnd once more, every 3rd rnd 2 times, every 2nd rnd 3 times, then every rnd 8 times—10 sts rem.

FINISHING

Break yarn, leaving an 8" (20.5 cm) tail. With tail threaded on a tapestry needle, draw through rem sts and pull tight. Fasten off on WS. Weave in loose ends.

SOLE

INSTEP

	ruby
	natural
	pattern repeat

NORDIC INSPIRATION 45

FAR EASTERN FLAIR

JAPAN

Sashiko embroidery emerged from the mending and embellishment of navy blue fishermen's clothing with white thread. Sashiko embroidery doesn't often appear in combination with knitting, but it is an especially pleasing traditional Japanese way to embellish a piece of knitting.

Finished size 8½" (21.5 cm) circumference and 9½ (10, 10½)" (24 [25.5, 26.5] cm) long from back of heel to tip of toe. To fit U.S. women's shoe sizes 5–6½ (7–8½, 9–10½) (European sizes 36–37 [38–39, 40–41]). Socks shown measure 10" (25.5 cm) long.

Yarn Fingering (Super Fine #1). *Shown here:* Regia 4-ply (75% wool, 25% nylon; 229 yd [209 m]/50 g): #1090 navy, 2 balls.

Needles U.S. size 1 (2.25 mm): set of 5 double-pointed (dpn). Adjust needle size if necessary to obtain the correct gauge.

Notions Marker (m); tapestry needle; 1 skein white embroidery floss; tissue or tracing paper; cardboard; straight pins.

Gauge 28 sts and 40 rnds = 4" (10 cm) in St st.

CUFF

CO 60 sts. Divide sts evenly onto 4 dpn, place marker (pm), and join for working in the rnd, being careful not to twist sts.

Work 15 rnds in cuff patt as foll: *K1 through back loop (tbl), p1; rep from *.

LEG

Change to St st and work until piece measures 7" (18 cm) from CO.

HEEL

Knit sts of Needle 1 onto Needle 4, keeping beg of rnd marker in place—30 sts on one needle. Heel will be worked back and forth using short-rows (see Glossary) over these 30 sts; rem sts will be worked later for instep.

HEEL BACK

SHORT-ROW 1 (set-up row) K15, turn.

SHORT-ROW 2 Slyo (see Glossary), p29, turn.

SHORT-ROW 3 Slyo, knit to slyo created on previous row, turn.

SHORT-ROW 4 Slyo, purl to slyo created on previous row, turn.

Rep Short-rows 3 and 4 eight more times, then work Short-row 3 once more, but do not turn—10 slyo sts at each end of heel, 10 plain sts in center.

Work to end of rnd in St st, working each slyo as 1 st. Work 1 more rnd even.

HEEL BASE

SHORT-ROW 1 (RS) Knit to last 9 heel sts, turn.

SHORT-ROW 2 Slyo, p11, turn.

SHORT-ROW 3 Slyo, knit to slyo created on previous row, knit slyo as 1 st, k1, turn.

SHORT-ROW 4 Slyo, purl to slyo created on previous row, purl slyo as 1 st, p1, turn.

Rep Short-rows 3 and 4 eight more times.

NEXT ROW Slyo, k14 (to end of rnd)—first and last sts of heel are slyos. Divide heel sts evenly onto 2 needles. Resume working in the rnd, working rem 2 slyo as 1 st on first rnd.

FOOT

Work even in St st until foot measures 7¼ (7¾, 8¼)" (18.5 [19.5, 21] cm) from back of heel.

TOE

DEC RND **NEEDLES 1 AND 3** Knit to last 3 sts, k2tog, k1; **NEEDLES 2 AND 4** K1, ssk, knit to end—4 sts dec'd.

Rep dec rnd every 4th rnd once more, every 3rd rnd 2 times, every 2nd rnd 3 times, then every rnd 6 times—8 sts rem.

FINISHING

Break yarn, leaving an 8" (20.5 cm) tail. With tail threaded on a tapestry needle, draw through rem sts and pull tight. Fasten off on WS. Weave in loose ends.

SASHIKO EMBROIDERY

Cut two pieces of cardboard 4" x 12" (10 x 30.5 cm). At one of the narrow ends, cut a rounded toe shape and insert in the toe of the sock; this will prevent stitching through both layers.

Trace the Sashiko drawing onto two pieces of tissue or tracing paper (one for each sock). Attach one paper pattern to each sock with straight pins. Separate embroidery floss into 6 strands, then work with 3 strands held tog. With about a yd (meter) of embroidery floss threaded on a tapestry needle, embroider over the pattern on the tissue (see Glossary). Follow the lines as closely as possible with the tip of the needle. Join more embroidery floss as needed. When motif is complete, remove the paper. Weave in loose ends.

LISTEN TO YOUR WANDERLUST

A rmenians live between the eastern part of Anatolia and the southern Caucasus. They were subjected to persecution and conquest during the last century, but they also maintained regular contact with European countries. Their designs reflect many cultural influences, including Christian symbolism.

Finished size 9½" (24 cm) foot circumference and 9½ (11¼, 11¾)" (24 [28.5, 30] cm) long from back of heel to tip of toe. To fit U.S. women's shoe sizes 5–6½ (7–8½, 9–10½) (European sizes 36–37 [38–39, 40–41]). Socks shown measure 11¼" (28.5 cm) long.

Yarn Fingering (Super Fine #1). *Shown here:* Regia 4-ply (75% wool, 25% nylon; 229 yd [209 m]/50 g): #1992 natural, #0522 charcoal, and #1230 sienna, 1 ball each.

Needles U.S. size 1 (2.25 mm): set of 5 double-pointed (dpn). Adjust needle size if necessary to obtain the correct gauge.

Notions Marker (m); tapestry needle.

Gauge 36 sts and 40 rnds = 4" (10 cm) in charted patt.

CUFF

With natural, CO 76 sts. Divide sts evenly onto 4 dpn, place marker (pm), and join for working in the rnd, being careful not to twist sts.

Work 20 rnds in rib as foll: *K1 through back loop (tbl), p1; rep from *.

NEXT RND (inc rnd) *K9, M1 (see Glossary); rep from * to last 4 sts, k4—84 sts.

LEG

Arrange sts evenly onto 3 dpn (28 sts on each needle). Beg and ending as indicated for leg, work Rows 1–28 of Leg chart once, then work Rows 1–14 once more. Break yarns.

HEEL

Place first 20 sts of rnd and last 21 sts of rnd onto one needle—41 sts. Heel will be worked back and forth in rows on these 41 sts with natural; rem sts will be worked later for instep. With RS facing, attach natural at beg of heel sts.

ROW 1 (RS; dec row) Sl 1 pwise with yarn in back (wyb), k2, *k2tog, k6; rep from * 3 more times, k2tog, k4—36 sts rem.

ROW 2 Sl 1 pwise with yarn in front (wyf), p35.

LEG

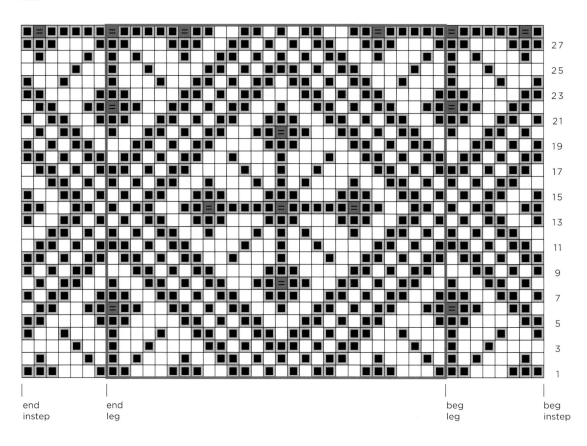

| | | | | | | | | | | 27 |
| 25 |
| 23 |
| 21 |
| 19 |
| 17 |
| 15 |
| 13 |
| 11 |
| 9 |
| 7 |
| 5 |
| 3 |
| 1 |

end instep   end leg   beg leg   beg instep

natural

charcoal

k2tog with charcoal

ssk with charcoal

knit with natural, then
duplicate st with sienna

pattern repeat

SOLE

1

HEEL FLAP

ROW 1 (RS) Sl 1 pwise wyb, *sl 1 pwise wyb, k1; rep from * to last st, k1.

ROW 2 Sl 1 pwise wyf, purl to end.

Rep Rows 1 and 2 sixteen more times.

TURN HEEL

Work short-rows (see Glossary) as foll:

SHORT-ROW 1 (RS) K19, ssk, k1, turn.

SHORT-ROW 2 Sl 1, p3, p2tog, p1, turn.

SHORT-ROW 3 Sl 1, knit to 1 st before gap created on previous row, ssk, k1, turn.

SHORT-ROW 4 Sl 1, purl to 1 st before gap created on previous row, p2tog, p1, turn.

Rep Short-rows 3 and 4 six more times—20 heel sts rem.

SHAPE GUSSETS

Pick up sts along selvedges of heel flap and rejoin for working in the rnd as foll:

RND 1 With natural, k20 heel sts, pick up and knit 17 sts along edge of heel flap (Needle 1); **NEEDLES 2 AND 3** Attach charcoal and, beg and ending as indicated for instep, work Row 15 of Leg chart, break charcoal; with another needle (Needle 4), pick up and knit 17 sts along other edge of heel flap, k10 heel sts from Needle 1, M1 (see Glossary)—98 sts total; 27 sts on Needle 1, 22 sts on Needle 2, 21 sts on Needle 3, and 28 sts on Needle 4.

RND 2 (sole set-up rnd) **NEEDLE 1** Work Row 2 of Sole chart to last 2 sts, k2 with charcoal; **NEEDLES 2 AND 3** Work Row 16 of Leg chart. Rnd begins at beg of Needle 4.

RND 3 NEEDLE 4 K2 with charcoal, work next row of Sole chart; **NEEDLE 1** Work Sole chart to last 2 sts, k2 with charcoal; **NEEDLES 2 AND 3** Work next row of Leg chart.

Rep Rnd 3 two more times.

NEXT RND (dec rnd) **NEEDLE 4** K1, ssk with charcoal, work in patt to end; **NEEDLE 1** Work in patt to last 3 sts, k2tog with charcoal, k1; **NEEDLES 2 AND 3** Work in patt—2 sts dec'd.

Rep last 4 rnds 2 more times—92 sts rem; 24 sts on Needle 1, 22 sts on Needle 2, 21 sts on Needle 3, and 25 sts on Needle 4.

FOOT

NEXT RND NEEDLES 4 AND 1 Work Row 1 of Sole Motif chart; **NEEDLES 2 AND 3** Work Row 1 of Leg chart.

Work in patt through Row 39 of Sole Motif chart—86 sts rem; 21 sts on Needles 1 and 3, 22 sts on Needles 2 and 4.

Work 0 (17, 23) rows in patt as foll: **NEEDLES 4 AND 1** Work Rows 38 and 39 of Sole Motif chart 0 (8, 11) times, then work Row 38 zero (one, one) more time; **NEEDLES 2 AND 3** Work Rows 12–28 of Leg chart 0 (1, 1) time, then work Rows 1–6 of chart 0 (0, 1) time. Cut charcoal.

TOE

RND 1 With natural, knit.

RND 2 (dec rnd) *K2tog, k2; rep from * to last 2 sts, k2tog—64 sts rem; 16 sts on each needle.

NEXT RND: (dec rnd) **NEEDLES 2 AND 4** K1, ssk, knit to end; **NEEDLES 1 AND 3** Knit to last 3 sts, k2tog, k1—4 sts dec'd.

Rep dec rnd every 4th rnd once more, every 3rd rnd 2 times, every 2nd rnd 3 times, then every rnd 7 times—8 sts rem.

FINISHING

Break yarn, leaving an 8" (20.5 cm) tail. Thread tail on a tapestry needle, draw through rem 8 sts, and pull tight. Fasten off on WS. With sienna, work duplicate st as shown on charts. Weave in loose ends.

SOLE MOTIF

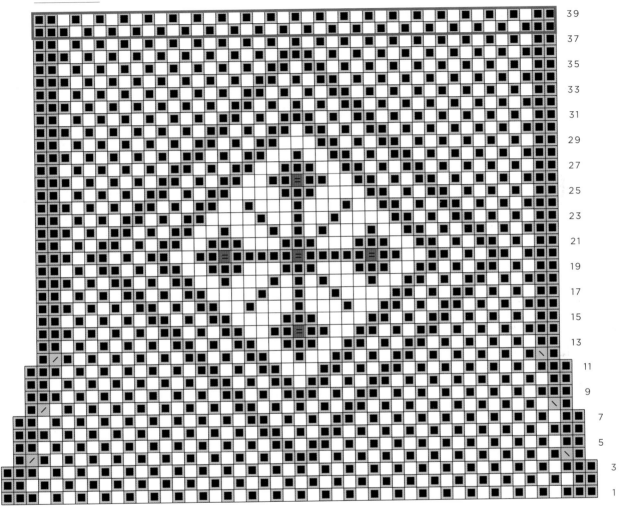

39
37
35
33
31
29
27
25
23
21
19
17
15
13
11
9
7
5
3
1

☐ natural

■ charcoal

╱ k2tog with charcoal

╲ ssk with charcoal

▦ knit with natural, then
duplicate st with sienna

☐ pattern repeat

FRANCONIAN BEADWORK

GERMANY

During its prime, bead knitting was viewed in central Europe as a specialized art knitting. It spread to Nurnberg, Bohemia, Venice, and mountain areas where the glass bead industry was established. Pouches, purses, cuffs, and socks were made with rich bead patterns and sold as desirable rarities.

Finished size 7½" (19 cm) circumference and 8¼ (8¾, 9¼)" (21 [22, 23.5] cm) long from back of heel to tip of toe. To fit U.S. women's shoe sizes 5–6½ (7–8½, 9–10½) (European sizes 36–37 [38–39, 40–41]). Socks shown measure 8¾" (22 cm) long.

Yarn Fingering (Super Fine #1). *Shown here:* Regia 4-ply (75% wool, 25% nylon; 229 yd [209 m]/50 g): #0152 light blue, 2 balls.

Needles U.S. size 1 (2.25 mm): set of 5 double-pointed (dpn). Adjust needle size if necessary to obtain the correct gauge.

Notions Marker (m); tapestry needle; 570 size 10° blue seed beads (about 16 g); sewing needle and thread.

Gauge 32 sts and 44 rnds = 4" (10 cm) in St st.

CUFF

Use sewing needle and thread to string 285 seed beads onto yarn (see Glossary).

CO 80 sts. Knit 2 rows. Arrange sts evenly onto 4 dpn, place marker (pm), and join for working in the rnd, being careful not to twist sts.

Work Rows 1–7 of Edging chart—60 sts rem.

Knit 3 rnds.

PEACOCK

RIGHT SOCK ONLY

RNDS 1–26 NEEDLES 1 AND 2 Work Peacock chart, *reading from right to left* (see Glossary for bead knitting); **NEEDLES 3 AND 4** Knit.

LEFT SOCK ONLY

RNDS 1–26 NEEDLES 1 AND 2 Knit; **NEEDLES 3 AND 4** Work Peacock chart, *reading from left to right*.

BOTH SOCKS

Knit 14 rnds.

HEEL

Knit 15 sts of Needle 1 onto Needle 4, keeping beg of rnd marker in place—30 sts on one needle. Heel will be worked back and forth using short-rows (see Glossary) over these 30 sts; rem sts will be worked later for instep.

HEEL BACK

SHORT-ROW 1 (WS) Slyo (see Glossary), p29, turn.

SHORT-ROW 2 Slyo, knit to slyo created on previous row, turn.

SHORT-ROW 3 Slyo, purl to slyo created on previous row, turn.

Rep Short-rows 2 and 3 eight more times, then work Short-row 2 once more but do not turn—10 slyo sts at each end of heel, 10 plain sts in center.

Knit to end of rnd, working each slyo as 1 st. Knit 1 more rnd even.

HEEL BASE

SHORT-ROW 1 (RS) Knit to last 9 sts of heel, turn.

SHORT-ROW 2 Slyo, p11, turn.

SHORT-ROW 3 Slyo, knit to slyo created on previous row, knit slyo as 1 st, k1, turn.

SHORT-ROW 4 Slyo, purl to slyo created on previous row, purl slyo as 1 st, p1, turn.

Rep Short-rows 3 and 4 eight more times.

NEXT ROW Slyo, k14 (to end of rnd). Resume working in the rnd.

FOOT

Work even in St st until foot measures 6¼ (6¾, 7¼)" (16 [17, 18.5] cm) from back of heel.

TOE

DEC RND NEEDLES 1 AND 3 Knit to last 3 sts, k2tog, k1; **NEEDLES 2 AND 4** K1, ssk, knit to end—4 sts dec'd.

Rep dec rnd every 4th rnd once more, every 3rd rnd 2 times, every 2nd rnd 3 times, then every rnd 6 times—8 sts rem.

FINISHING

Break yarn, leaving an 8" (20.5 cm) tail. With tail threaded on a tapestry needle, draw through rem sts and pull tight. Fasten off on WS. Weave in loose ends.

EDGING

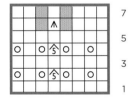

		7		
		5		
		3		
		1		

PEACOCK

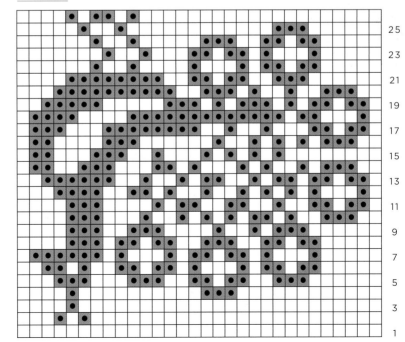

knit

◯ yo

Λ sl 2 as if to k2tog, k1, p2sso

↥ sl 3 as if to k3tog, k2tog, p3sso

no stitch

• place bead (see Glossary)

pattern repeat

BRUSSELS LACE

BELGIUM

During the time Brussels lace was produced in the Flemish region of Belgium, the influence of the French-speaking Wallonie region caused the wide spread of lace knitting. The delicate colors and transparent appearance make it extremely well-suited for romantic, feminine socks.

Finished size 7½ (7¾, 7¾)" (19 [19.5, 19.5] cm) foot circumference and 9¾ (10¼, 10¾)" (25 [26, 27.5] cm) long from back of heel to tip of toe. To fit U.S. women's shoe sizes 5–6½ (7–8½, 9–10½) (European sizes 36–37 [38–39, 40–41]). Socks shown measure 10¼" (26 cm) long.

Yarn Fingering (Super Fine #1). *Shown here:* Regia Silk 4-ply (55% wool, 25% nylon, 20% silk; 219 yd [200 m]/50 g): #0002 natural heather, 2 balls. (See Notes.)

Needles U.S. size 0 (2 mm) for smallest size, or U.S. size 1 (2.25 mm) for 2 larger sizes:

set of 5 double-pointed (dpn). Adjust needle size if necessary to obtain the correct gauge.

Notions Marker (m); tapestry needle; 66 clear silver-lined size 9° seed beads; sewing thread and needle.

Gauge 40 sts and 42 rnds = 4" (10 cm) in lace patt for smallest size; 39 sts and 40 rnds = 4" (10 cm) in lace patt for 2 larger sizes.

32 sts and 42 rnds = 4" (10 cm) in St st for smallest size; 30 sts and 40 rnds = 4" (10 cm) in St st for 2 larger sizes.

Note For U.S. women's shoe sizes 5–6½ (European sizes 36–37), choose 4-ply wool sock yarn that does not contain any silk or cotton.

CUFF

With sewing needle and thread, string 33 beads onto one ball of yarn (see Glossary) and push them up away from the end. Using the provisional method (see Glossary), CO 66 sts. Divide sts onto 4 dpn as foll: 16 sts on Needles 1 and 3, 17 sts on Needles 2 and 4. Place marker (pm) and join for working in the rnd, being careful not to twist sts.

Knit 7 rnds. Purl 1 rnd for turning ridge. Knit 3 rnds.

NEXT RND (bead rnd) Knit, adding beads (see Glossary) as foll: *Slide 1 bead up next to needle, k1 and pull bead through the old st (along with the new st), k1 without bead; rep from *.

NEXT RND *K1 through back loop (tbl), k1; rep from *.

Knit 2 rnds.

Fold fabric at purl rnd. Removing provisional CO as you go, *pick up first st of CO edge and place it onto left needle, k2tog (picked-up st with next st on needle); rep from * around—66 sts.

LEG

Rearrange sts evenly onto 3 dpn. Work Rows 1–28 of Lace chart 2 times.

HEEL SET-UP

Divide sts onto 4 needles and set up for heel as foll:

NEXT RND NEEDLE 1 K21; **NEEDLE 2** P1, work 16 sts according to chart Row 1; **NEEDLE 3** Cont in patt, work 17 sts according to chart Row 1; **NEEDLE 4** K11, then k5 from Needle 1 onto Needle 4 and pm for new beg of rnd—16 sts on each of Needles 1 and 4, 17 sts on each of Needles 2 and 3.

Work 7 more rnds in patt as established.

HEEL

Knit sts of Needle 1 onto Needle 4, keeping beg of rnd marker in place—32 sts total. Heel will be worked back and forth using short-rows (see Glossary) on these 32 sts; rem sts will be worked later for instep.

HEEL BACK

SHORT-ROW 1 (WS) Slyo (see Glossary), p31, turn.

SHORT-ROW 2 Slyo, knit to slyo created on previous row, turn.

SHORT-ROW 3 Slyo, purl to slyo created on previous row, turn.

Rep Short-rows 2 and 3 nine more times, then work Short-row 2 once more but do not turn—11 slyo sts at each end of heel, 10 plain sts in center.

FOOT

Resume working in the rnd over all sts as foll, working rem 2 slyo as 1 st on first rnd: **NEEDLES 1 AND 4 (SOLE)** Knit; **NEEDLES 2 AND 3 (INSTEP)** P1, work Lace chart.

Work in patt as established until sock measures 7¼ (7¾, 8¼)" (18.5 [19.5, 21] cm) from back of heel, ending with an even-numbered row of chart.

TOE

NEXT RND (set-up rnd) **NEEDLES 1 AND 4** Knit; **NEEDLE 2** K1, ssk, knit to end; **NEEDLE 3** Knit to last 3 sts, k2tog, k1—64 sts rem.

NEXT RND (dec rnd) **NEEDLES 1 AND 3** Knit to last 3 sts, k2tog, k1; **NEEDLES 2 AND 4** K1, ssk, knit to end—4 sts dec'd.

Rep dec rnd every 4th rnd once more, every 3rd rnd 2 times, every 2nd rnd 3 times, then every rnd 7 times—8 sts rem.

FINISHING

Cut yarn, leaving an 8" (20.5 cm) tail. With tail threaded on a tapestry needle, draw through rem sts and pull tight. Fasten off on WS. Weave in loose ends.

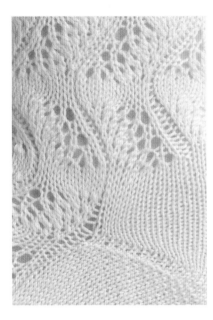

NEXT RND Knit to end of heel sts, being careful to work slyo as 1 st; **NEEDLES 2 AND 3** P1, work Row 9 of Lace chart; **HEEL STS** Knit to end of rnd, being careful to work slyo as one st. Work 1 more rnd even in patt.

HEEL BASE

Work back and forth using short-rows on heel sts as foll:

SHORT-ROW 1 (RS) Knit to last 10 sts of heel, turn.

SHORT-ROW 2 Slyo, p11, turn.

SHORT-ROW 3 Slyo, knit to slyo created on previous row, knit slyo as 1 st, k1, turn.

SHORT-ROW 4 Slyo, purl to slyo created on previous row, purl slyo as 1 st, p1, turn.

Rep Short-rows 3 and 4 nine more times. **NEXT ROW** Slyo, k15 (to end of rnd)—first and last sts of heel are slyos.

LACE

Chart legend:

- ☐ knit
- • purl
- ○ yo
- ╱ k2tog
- ╲ ssk
- ☐ pattern repeat

HUB OF FASHION

ITALY

Italian design is characterized by floral motifs and bright textured patterns, often worked in lively colors. The colorful knitwear of Missoni has made it one of the most beloved fashion houses in the world of fashion.

Finished size 8½" (21.5 cm) foot circumference and 10" (25.5 cm) long from back of heel to tip of toe. To fit U.S. women's shoe sizes 7–9 (European sizes 38–40).

Yarn Fingering (Super Fine #1). *Shown here:* Regia Design Line Kaffe Fassett (75% wool, 25% nylon; 229 yd [209 m]/50 g): #4350 landscape jungle, 2 balls.

Needles U.S. size 1 (2.25 mm): Two 16" (40 cm) or longer circular (cir) needles and set of 5 double-pointed

(dpn). Adjust needle size if necessary to obtain the correct gauge.

Notions Crochet hook (for provisional CO); waste cotton yarn in a contrasting color (for CO and edge sts); Scotch tape; markers (m); tapestry needle.

Gauge 30 sts and 40 rnds = 4" (10 cm) in St st.

Note This sock is worked from side to side. Work all edge sts as described for a smooth transition to toe and cuff.

STITCH GUIDE

Edge Stitches
Cut 2 lengths of waste yarn, each about 16" (40.5 cm) long. Wrap one end of each strand firmly with Scotch tape. At the end of each row, *work to last st in patt, M1 (see Glossary), work 1 st in St st and sl this st onto taped end of waste yarn.

INSTEP

Using the provisional method (see Glossary), CO 111 sts on 1 cir needle. Do not join. Purl 1 row.

Work Rows 1 and 2 of Zigzag chart 20 times—20 edge sts created for each length of waste yarn.

SOLE

NEXT ROW (RS; dec row) Work 54 sts according to Zigzag chart (end with k3tog), then work Zigzag Dec chart to end—100 sts rem.

Work 1 row even in patt.

GUSSET 1

Work short-rows (see Glossary) as foll:

SHORT-ROW 1 (RS) Work 49 sts according to Zigzag chart (end with yo, k1), place marker (pm), k25, turn.

SHORT-ROW 2 Slyo (see Glossary), purl to m, work in patt to end.

SHORT-ROW 3 Work in patt to m, k20, turn.

SHORT-ROW 4 Slyo, purl to m, work in patt to end.

SHORT-ROW 5 Work in patt to m, k15, turn.

SHORT-ROW 6 Slyo, purl to m, work in patt to end.

SHORT-ROW 7 Work in patt to m, k10, turn.

SHORT-ROW 8 Slyo, purl to m, work in patt to end.

SHORT-ROW 9 Work in patt to m, k5, turn.

SHORT-ROW 10 Slyo, purl to m, work in patt to end.

HEEL

Note: Work each slyo as 1 st when you come to it.

HEEL ROW 1 (RS) Work in patt to m, k3, M1, k1, pm, k2, M1, k3, pm, knit to last st, work edge st (see Stitch Guide)—102 sts.

HEEL ROW 2 AND ALL WS ROWS Purl to last m, work in patt to end.

HEEL ROW 3 (RS) Work in patt to m, k4, M1, k3, M1, k4, turn; slyo, purl to 2nd m, turn; slyo, knit to last st, work edge st—104 sts.

HEEL ROW 5 (RS) Work in patt to m, knit to 1 st before next m, M1, k3, M1, knit to last st, work edge st—2 sts inc'd.

HEEL ROW 7 (RS) Work in patt to m, knit to 1 st before next m, M1, k3, M1, knit to m, turn; slyo, purl to 2nd m, turn; slyo, knit to last st, work edge st—2 sts inc'd.

HEEL ROW 8 (WS) Purl to last m, work in patt to end.

HEEL ROWS 9–16 Rep Heel Rows 5–8 two more times—116 sts.

HEEL ROW 17 (RS) Work in patt to m, knit to last st, work edge st.

HEEL ROW 18 (WS) Purl to last m, work in patt to end.

HEEL ROWS 19–24 Rep Heel Rows 17 and 18 three more times.

ZIGZAG

ZIGZAG DECREASE

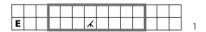

	k on RS; p on WS

	p1tbl on WS

	yo

	k2tog

	k3tog

	edge st (see Stitch Guide)

	pattern repeat

HEEL ROW 25 (RS) Work in patt to m, knit to 2 sts before next m, k2tog, k1, ssk, knit to m, turn; slyo, purl to 2nd m, turn; knit to last st, work edge st—114 sts rem.

HEEL ROW 27 (RS) Work in patt to m, knit to 2 sts before next m, k2tog, k1, ssk, knit to last st, work edge st—112 sts rem.

HEEL ROW 29 (RS) Work in patt to m, knit to 2 sts before next m, k2tog, k1, ssk, knit to m, turn; slyo, purl to 2nd m, turn; slyo, knit to last st, work edge st—2 sts dec'd.

HEEL ROW 31 (RS) Work in patt to m, knit to 2 sts before next m, k2tog, k1, ssk, knit to last st, work edge st—2 sts dec'd.

HEEL ROW 32 (WS) Purl to last m, work in patt to end.

Rep Heel Rows 29–32 two more times—100 sts rem.

GUSSET 2

SHORT-ROW 1 (RS) Work in patt to m (remove all markers foll this one as you come to them), k5, turn.

SHORT-ROW 2 (WS) Slyo, purl to m, work in patt to end.

SHORT-ROW 3 (RS) Work in patt to m, k10, turn.

SHORT-ROW 4 (WS) Slyo, purl to m, work in patt to end.

SHORT-ROW 5 (RS) Work in patt to m, k15, turn.

SHORT-ROW 6 (WS) Slyo, purl to m, work in patt to end.

SHORT-ROW 7 (RS) Work in patt to m, k20, turn.

SHORT-ROW 8 (WS) Slyo, purl to m, work in patt to end.

SHORT-ROW 9 (RS) Work in patt to m, k25, turn.

SHORT-ROW 10 (WS) Slyo, purl to m, work in patt to end.

NEXT ROW (RS) Work Zigzag chart to m, work Zigzag Inc chart to end—111 sts.

Work 1 row even in patt.

Cut yarn, leaving a 32" (81.5 cm) tail.

Remove provisional CO and place revealed sts onto second cir needle. Holding needles parallel, thread tail on a tapestry needle and use Kitchener st (see Glossary) to graft sts tog.

CUFF

Transfer 52 edge sts for cuff from waste yarn onto 4 dpn, dividing sts evenly.

NEXT RND *K6, M1, k7, M1; rep from *, working each knit st of rnd as foll: sl 1 pwise, lift loop around base of sl st and place onto left needle, return sl st to left needle, k2tog (lifted loop and sl st)—60 sts.

Work 15 rnds in k2, p2 rib. BO all sts loosely in patt.

TOE

Transfer 42 edge sts for toe from waste yarn onto 4 dpn as foll: 11 sts on Needles 1 and 3; 10 sts on Needles 2 and 4.

NEXT RND *K1, M1, [k2, M1] 10 times; rep from *, working each knit st of rnd as foll: pick up st wrapped around base of next st and place onto left needle, k2tog (picked-up st and next st)—64 sts.

Knit 1 rnd, dividing sts evenly on dpn.

NEXT RND (dec rnd) **NEEDLES 1 AND 3** Knit to last 3 sts, k2tog, k1; **NEEDLES 2 AND 4** K1, ssk, knit to end—4 sts dec'd.

Rep dec rnd every 4th rnd once more, every 3rd rnd 2 times, every 2nd rnd 3 times, then every rnd 7 times—8 sts rem.

FINISHING

Break yarn, leaving an 8" (20.5 cm) tail. With tail threaded on a tapestry needle, draw through rem sts and pull tight. Fasten off on WS. Weave in loose ends.

ZIGZAG INCREASE

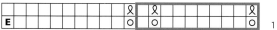

1

□ k on RS; p on WS

ຂ p1tbl on WS

○ yo

╱ k2tog

⅄ k3tog

E edge st (see Stitch Guide)

□ pattern repeat

TRADITIONAL COSTUME

AUSTRIA

Although Alpine regions require a warm, durable knitting, Vienna and the surrounding area became well-known for lace knitting. Motifs from everyday life such as flowers, trees, and animals are often knitted in cream, red, and dark green.

Finished size 8" (20.5 cm) circumference and 9¼" (23.5 cm) long from back of heel to tip of toe. To fit U.S. women's shoe sizes 7–9 (European sizes 38–40).

Yarn Fingering (Super Fine #1). *Shown here:* Regia 4-ply (75% wool, 25% nylon; 229 yd [209 m]/50 g): #1992 natural, #2002 cherry, and #0327 pine, 1 ball each.

Needles U.S. size 1 (2.25 mm): set of 5 double-pointed (dpn). Adjust needle size if necessary to obtain the correct gauge.

Notions U.S. size D/3 (3.25 mm) crochet hook; marker (m); waste yarn for provisional CO; tapestry needle.

Gauge 30 sts and 40 rnds = 4" (10 cm) in lace patt.

Notes This sock begins above the toe and is worked toward the cuff.

FOOT

With natural and using the provisional method (see Glossary), CO 60 sts. Divide sts evenly onto 4 dpn, place marker (pm), and join for working in the rnd, being careful not to twist sts. Knit 1 rnd.

NEXT RND NEEDLE 1 Knit (sole); **NEEDLES 2 AND 3** Work Lace chart (instep); **NEEDLE 4** Knit (sole).

Cont in patt, work Rows 1–20 of Lace chart 2 times.

HEEL

Heel is worked back and forth using short-rows (see Glossary) over 30 sts of Needles 1 and 4; rem 30 sts will be worked later for instep.

HEEL BASE

NEEDLE 1 Knit to end; turn. Sl sts from Needle 4 onto Needle 1, keeping beg of rnd marker in place.

SHORT-ROW 1 (WS) Slyo (see Glossary), p29, turn.

SHORT-ROW 2 Slyo, knit to slyo created on previous row, turn.

SHORT-ROW 3 Slyo, purl to slyo created on previous row, turn.

Rep Short-rows 2 and 3 eight more times, then work Short-row 2 once more but do not turn—10 slyo sts at each end of heel, 10 plain sts in center.

Knit to end of heel sts, being careful to work each slyo as one st, work Row 1 of

Lace chart across Needles 2 and 3, then knit to end of rnd, being careful to work each slyo as 1 st. Work 1 more rnd even, working Row 2 of Lace chart.

HEEL BACK

Work back and forth on 30 sts of heel as foll:

SHORT-ROW 1 (RS) Knit to last 9 heel sts, turn.

SHORT-ROW 2 Slyo, p11, turn.

SHORT-ROW 3 Slyo, knit to slyo created on previous row, knit slyo as 1 st, k1, turn.

SHORT-ROW 4 Slyo, purl to slyo created on previous row, purl slyo as 1 st, p1, turn.

Rep Short-rows 3 and 4 eight more times.

NEXT ROW Slyo, k14 (to end of rnd)— first and last sts of heel are slyos.

LEG

Resume working in the rnd, working rem 2 slyo as 1 st on first rnd.

NEXT RND NEEDLE 1 Knit; **NEEDLES 2 AND 3** Work Row 3 of Lace chart; **NEEDLE 4** Knit. Cont in patt for 7 more rnds.

Work Rows 11–20 of Lace chart over all sts.

Work Rows 1–10 of Tulip 1 chart.

Work Rows 1–10 of Lace chart.

Work Rows 1–10 of Tulip 2 chart. Knit 1 rnd.

CUFF

Work in k1 through back loop (tbl), p1 rib for 1½" (3.8 cm).

CROCHET PICOT BO

Sl first st onto crochet hook. Work 1 sc into next st, *ch 3, sl st into first ch of ch-3, sc into next 3 sts; rep from * to last st, ch 3, sl st into first ch of ch-3, sc into last st, join with sl st to beg sc. Fasten off.

TOE

Remove provisional CO and divide revealed sts evenly onto 4 dpn—60 sts. Attach natural.

NEXT RND (dec rnd) **NEEDLES 1 AND 3** Knit to last 3 sts, k2tog, k1; **NEEDLES 2 AND 4** K1, ssk, knit to end—4 sts dec'd.

Rep dec rnd every 4th rnd once more, every 3rd rnd 2 times, every 2nd rnd 3 times, then every rnd 6 times—8 sts rem.

FINISHING

Break yarn, leaving an 8" (20.5 cm) tail. With tail threaded on a tapestry needle, draw through rem sts and pull tight. Fasten off on WS. Weave in loose ends.

□	natural
+	cherry
=	pine
○	yo
∕	k2tog
∖	ssk
□	pattern repeat
⅄	knit into st 2 rows below with natural

LACE

TULIP 1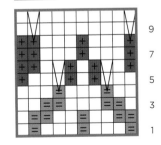

TULIP 2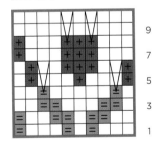

CLASSIC KILIM

TURKEY

raditional Turkish patterns use a rich blaze of color, and complex geometric shapes make such designs small works of art. Turkish socks are knitted toe-up with the final strand left to hang outside the sock and embellished with tassels and beads.

Finished size 8¾" (22 cm) circumference and 9¾" (25 cm) long from back of heel to tip of toe. To fit U.S. women's shoe sizes 7–9 (European sizes 38–40).

Yarn Fingering (Super Fine #1). *Shown here:* Regia Design Line Kaffe Fassett (75% wool, 25% nylon; 229 yd [209 m] /50 g): #4259 landscape fire, 2 balls. Regia 4-ply (75% wool, 25% nylon; 229 yd [209 m] /50 g): #1992 natural, 1 ball.

Needles U.S. size 1 (2.25 mm): set of 5 double-pointed (dpn). Adjust needle size if necessary to obtain the correct gauge.

Notions Marker (m); waste yarn for heel; tapestry needle.

Gauge 36 sts and 40 rnds = 4" (10 cm) in charted patt.

Note For braid, it is helpful to place the 2 balls of yarn about 1 yard (1 meter) away from you and continually slide the twist away from your work. In the rnds to come, the strands will untangle themselves.

Begin second sock at the same point in ball of multicolored yarn as first sock to match colors.

To keep from interrupting the complicated patterns of the heel, the heel is knitted later and lavishly decorated.

CUFF

With fire, CO 78 sts. Divide sts onto 4 dpn (20 sts on Needles 1 and 3, 19 sts on Needles 2 and 4), place marker (pm), and join for working in the rnd, being careful not to twist sts.

RND 1 *K1 with fire, k1 with natural; rep from *.

BRAID

Beg braid with both strands in front of work. Alternate strands as foll: take color to be knit to back of work, knit st, bring to front again.

RND 1 *K1 with fire, k1 with natural, always bringing the new yarn *under* the one just used; rep from *.

RND 2 *K1 with fire, k1 with natural, always bringing the new yarn *over* the one just used; rep from *.

LEG

Work Rows 1–18 of Leg chart, then work Rows 19–26 three times, then work Rows 27–36. Cut both strands.

PLACE HEEL

Sl 39 sts from Needles 4 and 1 onto waste yarn; sts will be worked later for heel. With natural and using the provisional method (see Glossary), CO 39 sts and divide onto Needles 1 and 4. Rnd beg between Needles 3 and 4.

FOOT

Work Rows 1–27 of Foot chart.

LEG

35
33
31
29
27
25
23
21
19
17
15
13
11
9
7
5
3
1

☐ natural

■ landscape fire

◪ k2tog with landscape fire

◪ ssk with landscape fire

M M1 with landscape fire

⊠ knit with landscape fire, then duplicate st

☐ pattern repeat

FOOT

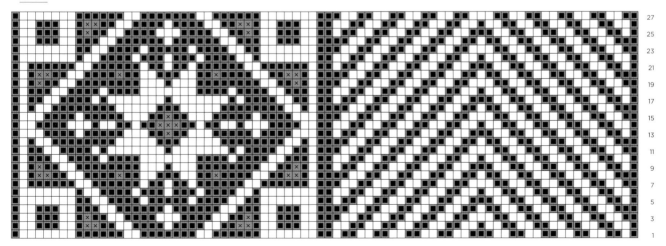

TOE

Work Rows 1–41 of Toe chart, twisting the 2 strands between Needles 3 and 4, and between Needles 1 and 2, so that the toe won't end up too narrow—6 sts rem.

Break yarns, leaving an 8" (20.5 cm) tail. With tail of fire threaded on a tapestry needle, draw through rem sts and pull tight. Fasten off both yarns on WS.

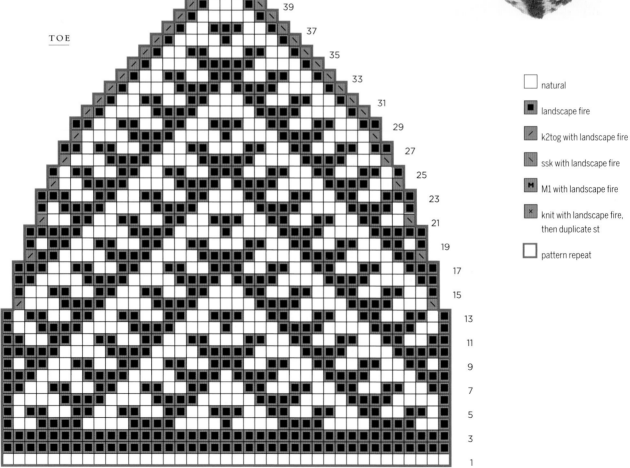

TOE

	natural
■	landscape fire
◢	k2tog with landscape fire
◸	ssk with landscape fire
M	M1 with landscape fire
×	knit with landscape fire, then duplicate st
	pattern repeat

HEEL

Remove provisional CO and divide 39 revealed sts onto 2 dpn (Needles 2 and 3). Replace 39 held sts onto 2 dpn (Needles 4 and 1); rnd beg between Needles 3 and 4. Attach fire and natural at beg of Needle 4.

NEXT RND (inc rnd) **NEEDLES 4 AND 2** M1 with fire, work Row 1 of Heel chart; **NEEDLES 1 AND 3** Cont Row 1 of Heel chart to end, M1 with fire—82 sts.

Work Rows 2–28 of Heel chart—10 sts rem. Break yarns, leaving an 8" (20.5 cm) tail. With tail of fire threaded on a tapestry needle, draw through rem sts and pull tight. Fasten off both yarns on WS.

FINISHING

EMBROIDERY

Cut a 32" (81.5 cm) length of fire in color to contrast with central motif on instep. With yarn threaded on a tapestry needle, use duplicate st to embroider as shown on Foot chart.

TASSELS

Cut twelve 6" (15 cm) long lengths of fire. Make 2 braids of 6 strands each and knot both ends. Make two 2" (5 cm) tassels of 30 strands each and attach one to each braid. Sew finished cord to side of CO edge.

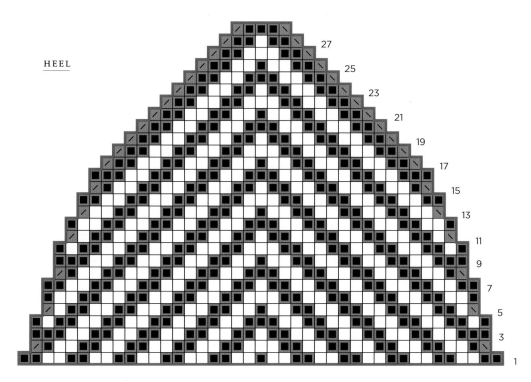

HEEL

IN THE HIGHLANDS

SCOTLAND

Argyle patterns can be traced back to the tartan patterns of the Campbell clan. Argyle is traditionally knitted in intarsia, so socks had to be seamed up when finished, but using short-rows avoids having to sew them later.

Finished size 8¼ (8½, 8½)" (21 [21.5, 21.5] cm) circumference and 9¾ (10¼, 10½)" (25 [26, 26.5] cm) long from back of heel to tip of toe. To fit U.S. women's shoe sizes 5–6½ (7–8½, 9–10½) (European sizes 36–37 [38–39, 40–41]). Socks shown measure 10¼" (26 cm) long.

Yarn Fingering (Super Fine #1). *Shown here:* Regia 4-ply (75% wool, 25% nylon; 229 yd [209 m]/50 g): #0522 charcoal and #2082 leaf, 1 ball each, and #1992 natural, about 2 yd (2 m).

Needles U.S. size 2 (2.75 mm): set of 5 double-pointed (dpn). Adjust needle size if necessary to obtain the correct gauge.

Notions Marker (m); tapestry needle.

Gauge 33 sts and 42 rnds = 4" (10 cm) in St st for smallest size; 32 sts and 40 rnds = 4" (10 cm) in St st for 2 larger sizes.

STITCH GUIDE

Upper Half of Diamond (worked over sts of 2 needles in color as indicated)

SHORT-ROW 1 (RS) K34, turn.

SHORT-ROW 2 Slyo (see Glossary), purl to end, turn.

SHORT-ROW 3 Slyo, knit to slyo created on previous row, turn.

SHORT-ROW 4 Slyo, purl to slyo created on previous row, turn.

Rep Short-rows 3 and 4 fifteen more times.

NEXT ROW Slyo—34 slyo sts.

Lower Half of Diamond (worked over sts of 2 needles in color as indicated)

Note: Beg Short-row 1 at center of sts for this diamond (e.g., if diamond is worked over Needles 4 and 1, beg Short-row 1 at beg of Needle 1).

SHORT-ROW 1 (RS) K1, turn.

SHORT-ROW 2 Slyo, p1, turn.

SHORT-ROW 3 Slyo, knit to slyo created on previous row, knit slyo as 1 st, k1, turn.

SHORT-ROW 4 Slyo, purl to slyo created on previous row, purl slyo as 1 st, p1, turn.

Rep Short-rows 3 and 4 fifteen more times—last st of row is slyo. *Note:* If lower half of diamond is followed by upper half of diamond, work first row of upper half of diamond as slyo, k33.

CUFF

With charcoal, CO 68 sts. Arrange sts evenly onto 4 dpn, place marker (pm), and join for working in the rnd, being careful not to twist sts.

Work in k1 through back loop (tbl), p1 rib for 14 rnds.

LEG

DIAMOND 1

NEEDLES 1 AND 2 With leaf, work an upper half of diamond (see Stitch Guide). Cut yarn.

NEEDLES 3 AND 4 With leaf, work an upper half of diamond.

NEEDLES 1–4 Knit 1 rnd over all sts, being careful to work each slyo as 1 st. Cut yarn.

NEEDLES 4 AND 1 With charcoal, work a lower half of diamond (see Stitch Guide), then an upper half of diamond. Cut yarn.

NEEDLES 2 AND 3 With charcoal, work a lower half of diamond, then an upper half of diamond.

NEEDLES 1–4 Knit 1 rnd over all sts, being careful to work each slyo as 1 st. Cut yarn.

DIAMOND 2

NEEDLES 1 AND 2 With leaf, work a lower half of diamond, then an upper half of diamond. Knit to end of Needle 2, turn, purl to end of Needle 1, being careful to work each slyo as 1 st. Cut yarn.

NEEDLES 3 AND 4 With leaf, work a lower half of diamond only. Cut yarn.

HEEL

Note: Work slyo as 1 st when you come to it.

Place 17 sts from Needle 3 and 17 sts from Needle 4 onto one needle—34 sts total. Heel will be worked back and forth with charcoal over these 34 sts; rem 34 sts will be worked later for instep.

NEXT ROW (RS) Sl 1 pwise, *k1, sl 1 pwise with yarn in back (wyb); rep from * to last st, k1.

NEXT ROW Sl 1 pwise, purl to end.

Rep last 2 rows 16 more times.

TURN HEEL

Work short-rows as foll:

SHORT-ROW 1 (RS) K19, ssk, k1, turn.

SHORT-ROW 2 Sl 1, p5, p2tog, p1, turn.

SHORT-ROW 3 Sl 1, knit to 1 st before gap created on previous row, ssk, k1, turn.

SHORT-ROW 4 Sl 1, purl to 1 st before gap created on previous row, p2tog, p1, turn.

Rep Short-rows 3 and 4 five more times—20 heel sts rem. Cut yarn.

SHAPE GUSSET

NEXT ROW With charcoal, RS facing, and one needle (Needle 3), pick up and knit 17 sts along right edge of heel flap, k10 heel sts; with another needle (Needle 4), k10 heel sts, pick up and knit 17 sts along left edge of heel flap; **NEEDLE 1** K1, turn—88 sts total.

NEXT ROW (WS) **NEEDLE 1** Slyo; **NEEDLES 4 AND 3** Purl; **NEEDLE 2** P1, turn.

NEXT ROW (RS) **NEEDLE 2** Slyo; **NEEDLE 3** K1, ssk, knit to end; **NEEDLE 4** Knit to last 3 sts, k2tog, k1; **NEEDLE 1** Knit slyo as 1 st, k1, turn—86 sts rem.

NEXT ROW (WS) **NEEDLE 1** Slyo, purl to end; **NEEDLES 4 AND 3** Purl; **NEEDLE 2** Purl to slyo created on previous row, purl slyo as 1 st, p1, turn.

NEXT ROW **NEEDLE 2** Slyo, knit to end; **NEEDLE 3** K1, ssk, knit to end; **NEEDLE 4** Knit to last 3 sts, k2tog, k1; **NEEDLE 1** Knit to slyo created on previous row, knit slyo as 1 st, k1, turn—2 sts dec'd.

Rep last 2 rows 8 more times, then work WS row once more—68 sts rem.

FOOT

NEXT ROW (RS) **NEEDLE 2** Slyo, knit to end; **NEEDLES 3 AND 4** Knit; **NEEDLE 1** Knit to slyo created on previous row, knit slyo as 1 st, k1, turn.

NEXT ROW **NEEDLE 1** Slyo, purl to end; **NEEDLES 4 AND 3** Purl; **NEEDLE 2** Purl to slyo created on previous row, purl slyo as 1 st, p1, turn.

Rep last 2 rows 5 more times.

NEXT ROW Slyo, knit to end of Needle 4—last st of Needle 1 and first st of Needle 2 are slyos.

Resume working in the rnd.

NEXT RND Knit, being careful to work each slyo as 1 st. Work even until foot measures 7½ (8, 8¼)" (19 [20.5, 21] cm) from back of heel.

TOE

NEXT RND (dec rnd) **NEEDLES 1 AND 3** K1, ssk, knit to end; **NEEDLES 2 AND 4** Knit to last 3 sts, k2tog, k1—4 sts dec'd.

Rep dec rnd every 4th rnd once more, every 3rd rnd 2 times, every 2nd rnd 3 times, then every rnd 8 times—8 sts rem.

FINISHING

Break yarn, leaving an 8" (20.5 cm) tail. With tail threaded on a tapestry needle, draw through rem sts and pull tight. Fasten off on WS.

EMBROIDERY

With natural threaded on a tapestry needle, use a running st to embroider diagonal lines through each diamond as shown, with each visible st covering about 1 knit st. Weave in loose ends.

KNIT SAMPLER

ENGLAND

The British Isles are home to a large variety of knitting patterns, incorporating the techniques of Western Europe and North Africa. As a result, a rich treasury of expressive patterns developed, including the typical tree of life motif featured here.

Finished size 8 (8¼, 8¼)" (20.5 [21, 21] cm) foot circumference and 9¼ (9¾, 10¼)" (23.5 [25, 26] cm) long from back of heel to tip of toe. To fit U.S. women's shoe sizes 5–6½ (7–8½, 9–10½) (European sizes 36–37 [38–39, 40–41]). Socks shown measure 9¾" (25 cm) long.

Yarn Fingering (Super Fine #1). *Shown here:* Regia Silk 4-ply (55% wool, 25% nylon, 20% silk; 219 yd [200 m]/50 g): #0012 camel, 2 balls. (See Notes.)

Needles U.S. size 0 (2 mm) for smallest size, or U.S. size 1 (2.25 mm) for 2 larger sizes:

set of 5 double-pointed (dpn). Adjust needle size if necessary to obtain the correct gauge.

Notions Marker (m); cable needle (cn); tapestry needle.

Gauge 33 sts and 42 rnds = 4" (10 cm) in St st for smallest size; 32 sts and 40 rnds = 4" (10 cm) in St st for 2 larger sizes.

Notes On the Foot chart, work the cable crosses fairly tightly so that they will be visible on the foot.

For U.S. women's shoe sizes 5–6½ (European sizes 36–37), use a 100% wool yarn.

SHORT-ROW 4 Slyo, purl to slyo created on previous row, purl slyo as 1 st, p1, turn.

Rep Short-rows 3 and 4 nine more times.

NEXT ROW Slyo, k16 (to end of Needle 3)—first and last sts of heel are slyos.

FOOT

Resume working in the rnd, working rem 2 slyo as 1 st on first rnd. Knit to end of Needle 4.

NEXT RND **NEEDLES 1 AND 2** Work Row 1 of Instep chart; **NEEDLES 3 AND 4** Knit.

Work in patt as established until foot measures 7¼ (7¾, 8¼)" (18.5 [19.5, 21] cm) from back of heel.

TOE

NEXT RND (dec rnd) **NEEDLES 1 AND 2** Knit; **NEEDLE 3** K1, ssk, k14; **NEEDLE 4** K14, k2tog, k1—64 sts rem.

NEXT RND (dec rnd) **NEEDLES 1 AND 3** K1, ssk, knit to end; **NEEDLES 2 AND 4** Knit to last 3 sts, k2tog, k1—4 sts dec'd.

Rep last rnd every 4th rnd once more, every 3rd rnd 2 times, every 2nd rnd 3 times, then every rnd 7 times—8 sts rem.

FINISHING

Break yarn, leaving an 8" (20.5 cm) tail. With tail threaded on a tapestry needle, draw through rem sts and pull tight. Fasten off on WS. Weave in loose ends.

CUFF

CO 74 sts. Arrange sts onto 4 dpn (19 sts each on Needles 1 and 3, 18 sts each on Needles 2 and 4), place marker (pm), and join for working in the rnd, being careful not to twist sts. Work 12 rnds in k1 through back loop (tbl), p1 rib.

LEG

Work Rows 1–42 of Leg chart—66 sts rem. Purl 1 rnd. Knit 3 rnds.

Work Rows 1–10 of Lattice chart. Knit 1 rnd.

NEXT RND **NEEDLES 1 AND 2** Purl; **NEEDLE 3** Knit; **NEEDLE 4** Knit to end, then k1 from Needle 1, turn—16 sts each on Needles 1 and 2; 17 sts each on Needles 3 and 4.

HEEL

Heel is worked back and forth using short-rows (see Glossary) over 34 sts of Needles 3 and 4; rem 32 sts will be worked later for instep. Rnd begins at beg of Needle 3.

HEEL TOP

SHORT-ROW 1 (WS) Slyo (see Glossary), purl to end, turn.

SHORT-ROW 2 Slyo, knit to slyo created on previous row, knit slyo as 1 st, turn.

SHORT-ROW 3 Slyo, purl to slyo created on previous row, purl slyo as 1 st, turn.

Rep Short-rows 2 and 3 nine more times, then work Short-row 2 once more—11 slyo sts at each end of heel, 12 plain sts in center.

Resume working in the rnd on all 4 needles as foll: **NEEDLES 1 AND 2** Knit; **NEEDLES 3 AND 4** Knit, being sure to work slyos as 1 st. Knit to end of Needle 2.

HEEL BOTTOM

Work back and forth on 34 sts of Needles 3 and 4 as foll:

SHORT-ROW 1 (RS) K24, turn.

SHORT-ROW 2 Slyo, p13, turn.

SHORT-ROW 3 Slyo, knit to slyo created on previous row, knit slyo as 1 st, k1, turn.

LEG

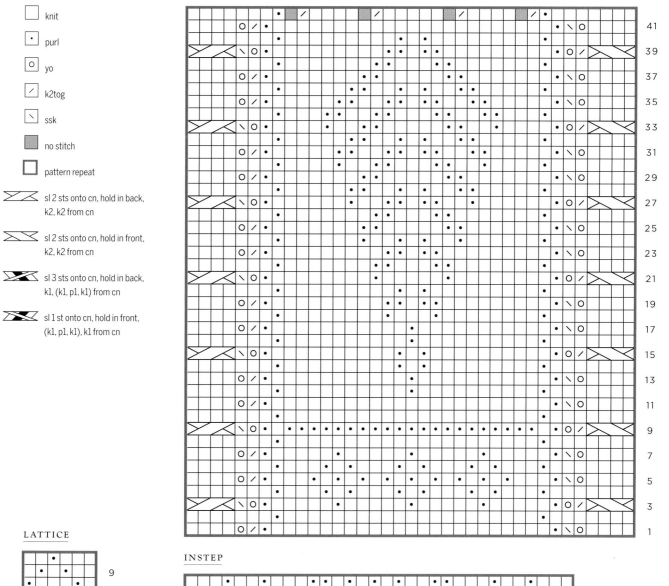

Legend:

- □ knit
- · purl
- ○ yo
- ╱ k2tog
- ╲ ssk
- ▨ no stitch
- □ pattern repeat
- ⬚ sl 2 sts onto cn, hold in back, k2, k2 from cn
- ⬚ sl 2 sts onto cn, hold in front, k2, k2 from cn
- ⬚ sl 3 sts onto cn, hold in back, k1, (k1, p1, k1) from cn
- ⬚ sl 1 st onto cn, hold in front, (k1, p1, k1), k1 from cn

LATTICE

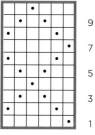

INSTEP

ON THE
ARAN ISLE

ARAN ISLE

IRELAND

The Aran Isles are well-known for the striking cables of their fishermen's sweaters. The patterns often serve as local or regional identification, and the wearer's initials were often worked into the bottom of the garment.

Finished size 8 (8½, 8½)" (20.5 [21.5, 21.5] cm) foot circumference and 9½ (10, 10½)" (24 [25.5, 26.5] cm) long from back of heel to tip of toe. To fit U.S. women's shoe sizes 5–6½ (7–8½, 9–10½) (European sizes 36–37 [38–39, 40–41]). Socks shown measure 10" (25.5 cm) long.

Yarn Fingering (Super Fine #1). *Shown here:* Regia 4-ply (75% wool, 25% nylon; 229 yd [209 m]/50 g): #1078 cardinal, 2 balls.

Needles U.S. size 0 (2 mm) for smallest size, or U.S. size 1 (2.25 mm) for 2 larger sizes: set of 5 double-pointed (dpn). Adjust needle size if necessary to obtain the correct gauge.

Notions Marker (m); cable needle (cn); waste yarn for provisional CO; tapestry needle.

Gauge 35 sts and 42 rnds = 4" (10 cm) in leg patt for smallest size; 34 sts and 40 rnds = 4" (10 cm) in leg patt for 2 larger sizes.

32 sts and 42 rnds = 4" (10 cm) in St st for smallest size; 30 sts and 42 rnds = 4" (10 cm) in St st for 2 larger sizes.

HEM

Using the provisional method (see Glossary), CO 72 sts. Arrange sts evenly onto 4 dpn, place marker (pm), and join for working in the rnd, being careful not to twist sts. Knit 3 rnds.

NEXT RND *Yo, k2tog; rep from * to end. Knit 3 rnds.

Join hem as foll: Fold fabric WS tog at yo rnd. Removing provisional CO as you go, *pick up first st of CO edge and place it onto left needle; k2tog (picked-up st with next st on needle); rep from * around—72 sts.

LEG

Work Rows 1–12 of Leg chart. At end of Row 12, shift beg of rnd as foll: use Needle 4 to p1 from Needle 1—17 sts on Needle 1, 18 sts each on Needles 2 and 3, 19 sts on Needle 4.

Work Row 13 and at the same time arrange sts evenly onto 4 dpn.

Work Rows 14–42 of Leg chart, then work Rows 15–35 once more.

NEXT RND (chart row 36) **NEEDLE 1** Work 14 sts of Leg chart; **NEEDLE 2** Work 4 rem sts from Needle 1 according to Leg chart, then work next 14 sts according to Leg chart; **NEEDLE 3** Work 4 rem sts from Needle 2 according to Leg chart, then work next 14 sts according to Leg chart; do not finish rnd.

HEEL

Place rem 4 sts from Needle 3, 18 sts from Needle 4, and 14 sts from Needle 1 onto one needle—36 sts total. Heel will be worked back and forth in rows on these 36 sts; rem 36 sts will be worked later for instep.

HEEL FLAP

ROW 1 (RS) Knit.

ROW 2 K3, p30, k3.

Rep Rows 1 and 2 seventeen more times.

TURN HEEL

Work short-rows (see Glossary) as foll:

SHORT-ROW 1 (RS) K19, ssk, k1, turn.

SHORT-ROW 2 Sl 1, p3, p2tog, p1, turn.

SHORT-ROW 3 Sl 1, knit to 1 st before gap created on previous row, ssk, k1, turn.

LEG

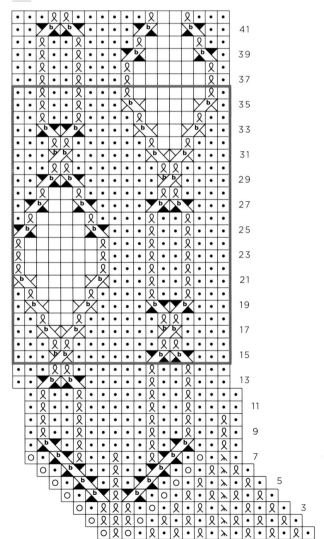

SHORT-ROW 4 Sl 1, purl to 1 st before gap created on previous row, p2tog, p1, turn.

Rep Short-rows 3 and 4 six more times—20 heel sts rem.

SHAPE GUSSET

NEXT RND With one needle (Needle 1), k20 heel sts, pick up and knit 18 sts along edge of heel flap; work Row 1 of Foot chart over next 36 sts (Needles 2 and 3); with another needle (Needle 4), pick up and knit 18 sts along edge of heel flap, k10 from Needle 1—92 sts total; 28 sts each on Needles 1 and 4, 18 sts each on Needles 2 and 3.

NEXT ROW NEEDLE 1 Knit; **NEEDLES 2 AND 3** Work Row 2 of Foot chart; **NEEDLE 4** Knit. Work 2 rnds in patt as established.

NEXT RND (dec rnd) **NEEDLE 1** Knit to last 3 sts, k2tog, k1; **NEEDLES 2 AND 3** Work in patt as established; **NEEDLE 4** K1, ssk, knit to end—2 sts dec'd.

Rep last 3 rnds 11 more times—68 sts rem; 16 sts each on Needles 1 and 4, 18 sts each on Needles 2 and 3.

FOOT

Work even in patt as established until foot measures 7¼ (7¾, 8¼)" (18.5 [19.5, 21] cm) from back of heel.

NEXT RND NEEDLE 1 Knit; **NEEDLE 2** K5, k2tog, k6, k2tog, k3; **NEEDLE 3** K3, k2tog, k6, k2tog, k5; **NEEDLE 4** Knit—64 sts rem. Knit 1 rnd.

TOE

NEXT RND (dec rnd) **NEEDLES 1 AND 3** Knit to last 3 sts, k2tog, k1; **NEEDLES 2 AND 4** K1, ssk, knit to end—4 sts dec'd.

Rep dec rnd every 4th rnd once more, every 3rd rnd 2 times, every 2nd rnd 3 times, then every rnd 7 times—8 sts rem.

FINISHING

Break yarn, leaving an 8" (20.5 cm) tail. With tail threaded on a tapestry needle, draw through rem sts and pull tight. Fasten off on WS. Weave in loose ends.

knit

purl

k1tbl

yo

sssk

pattern repeat

sl 1 st onto cn, hold in back, k1tbl, k1 from cn

sl 1 st onto cn, hold in front, k1, k1tbl from cn

sl 1 st onto cn, hold in back, k1tbl, k1tbl from cn

sl 1 st onto cn, hold in back, k1tbl, p1 from cn

sl 1 st onto cn, hold in front, p1, k1tbl from cn

FOOT

IT'S TEA TIME

ENGLAND

The textured patterns found on English fishermen's sweaters are made up of knit and purl stitches that are often combined with simple cables. The interplay of these patterns also appears frequently on socks.

Finished size 8½" (21.5 cm) circumference and 10 (10½, 10¾)" (25.5 [26.5, 27.5] cm) long from back of heel to tip of toe. To fit U.S. women's shoe sizes 5–6½ (7–8½, 9–10½) (European sizes 36–37 [38–39, 40–41]). Socks shown measure 10½" (26.5 cm) long.

Yarn Fingering (Super Fine #1). *Shown here:* Regia 4-ply (75% wool, 25% nylon; 229 yd [209 m]/50 g): #2190 beech fruit (celery), 2 balls.

Needles U.S. size 1 (2.25 mm): set of 5 double-pointed (dpn). Adjust needle size if necessary to obtain the correct gauge.

Notions Marker (m); cable needle (cn); tapestry needle.

Gauge 35 sts and 40 rnds = 4" (10 cm) in charted patt.

STITCH GUIDE

Seed stitch
(multiple of 2 sts)

RND 1 *K1, p1; rep from *.

RND 2 Knit the purl sts and purl the knit sts.

Rep Rnd 2 for patt.

CUFF

CO 72 sts. Arrange sts evenly onto 4 dpn, place marker (pm), and join for working in the rnd, being careful not to twist sts.

Work in k1 through back loop (tbl), p1 rib for 16 rnds.

LEG

Note: Be sure not to work texture patt too loosely; use a smaller size needle if necessary.

Work Leg chart and at the same time inc 2 sts on 2nd rnd as foll:

RND 1 *Work Row 1 of Leg chart, skipping first st of chart; rep from * once more.

RND 2 *Work first st of Row 2 of chart, M1 (see Glossary), skip 2nd st of chart, work Row 2 to end; rep from * once more—74 sts.

Work Rows 3–8 of Leg chart, then rep Rows 1–8 of chart until piece measures about 7¼" (18.5 cm) from CO, ending with Row 8 of chart.

HEEL

Place first 37 sts of rnd onto one needle—37 sts total. Heel will be worked back and forth in rows on these 37 sts; rem 37 sts will be worked later for instep. Work Rows 1–8 of Heel Flap chart 4 times.

TURN HEEL

Work short-rows (see Glossary) as foll:

SHORT-ROW 1 (RS) K20, ssk, k1, turn.

SHORT-ROW 2 Sl 1, p4, p2tog, p1, turn.

SHORT-ROW 3 Sl 1, knit to 1 st before gap created on previous row, ssk, k1, turn.

SHORT-ROW 4 Sl 1, purl to 1 st before gap created on previous row, p2tog, p1, turn.

Rep Short-rows 3 and 4 six more times—21 heel sts rem.

SHAPE GUSSET

NEXT RND With one needle (Needle 1), k21 heel sts, pick up and knit 16 sts along edge of heel flap; work Row 1 of Leg chart (Needles 2 and 3); with another needle (Needle 4), pick up and knit 16 sts along other edge of heel flap, k11 from Needle 1—90 sts total; 26 sts on Needle 1, 19 sts on Needle 2, 18 sts on Needle 3, 27 sts on Needle 4.

NEXT RND NEEDLE 1 K16, work in seed st (see Stitch Guide) to last 2 sts, k2; **NEEDLES 2 AND 3** Work next row of Leg chart; **NEEDLE 4** K2, work in seed st to last 17 sts, k17.

Rep last rnd 2 more times.

NEXT RND (dec rnd) **NEEDLE 1** K16, work in seed st to last 3 sts, k2tog, k1; **NEEDLES 2 AND 3** Work next row of Leg chart; **NEEDLE 4** K1, ssk, work in seed st to last 17 sts, k17—2 sts dec'd.

Rep last 3 rnds 7 more times—74 sts rem.

FOOT

Work even in patt as established until foot measures about 7½ (8, 8¼)" (19 [20.5, 21] cm) from back of heel, ending with Row 8 of Leg chart.

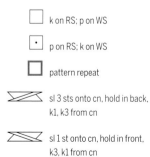

☐ k on RS; p on WS

• p on RS; k on WS

☐ pattern repeat

sl 3 sts onto cn, hold in back, k1, k3 from cn

sl 1 st onto cn, hold in front, k3, k1 from cn

LEG

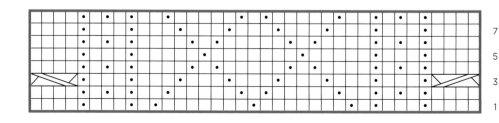

TOE

NEXT RND (dec rnd) **NEEDLES 1 AND 3** Knit; **NEEDLES 2 AND 4** Ssk, knit to end—72 sts rem.

NEXT RND (dec rnd) **NEEDLES 1 AND 3** Knit to last 3 sts, k2tog, k1; **NEEDLES 2 AND 4** K1, ssk, knit to end—4 sts dec'd.

Rep last rnd every 4th rnd once more, every 3rd rnd 2 times, every 2nd rnd 3 times, then every rnd 3 times—32 sts rem.

NEXT RND **NEEDLES 1 AND 3** Knit to last 2 sts, k2tog; **NEEDLES 2 AND 4** Ssk, knit to end—28 sts rem.

Knit sts on Needle 1.

FINISHING

Sl sts from Needle 4 onto Needle 1 and from Needle 3 onto Needle 2. Cut yarn, leaving a 24" (61 cm) tail. With tail threaded on a tapestry needle, use Kitchener st (see Glossary) to graft rem sts tog. Weave in loose ends.

HEEL FLAP

GREEN ISLE

IRELAND

The three-leaf clover is the national symbol of Ireland. Legend has it that St. Patrick used it as a symbol to teach the Christian idea of the Trinity. Diamond patterns are found in textured knitting as well as stranded knitting.

Finished size 8¼ (8¾, 8¾)" (21 [22, 22] cm) circumference and 9¼ (9½, 10)" (23.5 [24, 25.5] cm) long from back of heel to tip of toe. To fit U.S. women's shoe sizes 5–6½ (7–8½, 9–10½) (European sizes 36–37 [38–39, 40–41]). Socks shown measure 9½" (24 cm) long.

YARN Fingering (Super Fine #1). *Shown here:* Regia 4-ply (75% wool, 25% nylon; 229 yd [209 m]/50 g): #1076 pink and #2082 leaf, 1 ball each.

Needles U.S. size 1 (2.25 mm) for smallest size, or U.S. size 2 (2.75 mm) for 2 larger sizes: set of 5 double-pointed (dpn) (see Notes). Adjust needle size if necessary to obtain the correct gauge.

Notions Marker (m); tapestry needle.

Gauge 36 sts and 42 rnds = 4" (10 cm) in charted patt for smallest size; 34 sts and 40 rnds = 4" (10 cm) in charted patt for 2 larger sizes.

Notes Due to the large pattern repeat, this design lends itself to being worked on 2 circular needles instead of double-pointed needles.

CUFF

With leaf, CO 64 sts. Arrange sts evenly onto 4 dpn, place marker (pm), and join for working in the rnd, being careful not to twist sts.

Purl 1 rnd. Knit 1 rnd. Work in k3, p1 rib for 16 rnds.

LEG

NEXT RND *K6, M1 (see Glossary); rep from * to last 4 sts, k4—74 sts; 19 sts on Needles 1 and 3, 18 sts on Needles 2 and 4. K19 sts of Needle 1; rnd beg with Needle 2.

Work Rows 1–10 of Leg chart 4 times.

HEEL

Place sts from Needles 1 and 4 onto one needle—37 sts total. Heel will be worked back and forth in rows on these 37 sts; rem 37 sts will be worked later for instep.

HEEL FLAP

Beg with a WS row, work in St st for 33 rows.

TURN HEEL

Work short-rows (see Glossary) as foll:

SHORT-ROW 1 (RS) K20, ssk, k1, turn.

SHORT-ROW 2 Sl 1, p4, p2tog, p1, turn.

SHORT-ROW 3 Sl 1, knit to 1 st before gap created on previous row, ssk, k1, turn.

SHORT-ROW 4 Sl 1, purl to 1 st before gap created on previous row, p2tog, p1, turn.

Rep Short-rows 3 and 4 six more times—21 heel sts rem.

SHAPE GUSSET

NEXT RND With RS facing and empty needle (Needle 1), k21 heel sts, pick up and knit 16 sts along edge of heel flap; work Row 1 of Leg chart, break pink (Needles 2 and 3); with another needle (Needle 4), pick up and knit 16 sts along other edge of heel flap, k10 from Needle 1—90 sts total. Sl last st of Needle 1 to Needle 2 and sl first st of Needle 4 to Needle 3—26 sts on Needle 1, 19 sts on Needle 2, 20 sts on Needle 3, 25 sts on Needle 4.

NEXT RND NEEDLE 1 *K1 with pink, k3 with leaf; rep from * 5 more times, k1 with pink, k1 with leaf; **NEEDLES 2 AND 3** Work Row 2 of Instep chart; **NEEDLE 4** K1 with leaf, *k1 with pink, k3 with leaf; rep from * 5 more times.

Work 2 rnds in patt as established, working sts on Needles 1 and 4 in colors as they appear.

NEXT RND (dec rnd) **NEEDLE 1** Work in patt to last 3 sts, k2tog with pink, k1 with leaf; **NEEDLES 2 AND 3** Work next row of Instep chart; **NEEDLE 4** K1 with leaf, ssk with pink, work in patt to end—2 sts dec'd.

Rep last 3 rnds 7 more times; last dec rnd falls on Row 6 of Instep chart—74 sts rem; 18 sts on Needle 1, 19 sts on Needle 2, 20 sts on Needle 3, 17 sts on Needle 4.

FOOT

Work even in patt until foot measures about 7¼ (7½, 8)" (18.5 [19, 20.5] cm) from back of heel. Break pink. Sl first st of Needle 2 to Needle 1 and sl last st of Needle 3 to Needle 4—19 sts on Needles 1 and 3, 18 sts on Needles 2 and 4.

TOE

NEXT RND (dec rnd) **NEEDLES 1 AND 3** K2tog, k10, k2tog, k5; **NEEDLES 2 AND 4** K6, k2tog, k10—68 sts rem.

NEXT RND (dec rnd) **NEEDLES 1 AND 3** Knit to last 3 sts, k2tog, k1; **NEEDLES 2 AND 4** K1, ssk, knit to end—4 sts dec'd.

Rep dec rnd every 4th rnd once more, every 3rd rnd 2 times, every 2nd rnd 3 times, then every rnd 8 times—8 sts rem.

FINISHING

Break yarn, leaving an 8" (20.5 cm) tail. With tail threaded on a tapestry needle, draw through rem sts and pull tight. Fasten off on WS. Weave in loose ends.

LEG

INSTEP

☐ pink

⊠ leaf

☐ pattern repeat

VACATION IN THE MOUNTAINS

SWITZERLAND

The Alpine influence appears in Swiss knitting in the prevalence of traveling stitches, worked literally with a twist. Richly patterned stockings are an important part of the traditional costume of both men and women.

Finished size 7¾ (8, 8)" (19.5 [20.5, 20.5] cm) foot circumference and 9¼ (9½, 10)" (23.5 [24, 25.5] cm) long from back of heel to tip of toe. To fit U.S. women's shoe sizes 5–6½ (7–8½, 9–10½) (European sizes 36–37 [38–39, 40–41]). Socks shown measure 9½" (24 cm) long.

Yarn Fingering (Super Fine #1). *Shown here:* Regia 4-ply (75% wool, 25% nylon; 229 yd [209 m]/50 g): #1230 sienna, 2 balls.

Needles U.S. size 0 (2 mm) for smallest size, or U.S. size 1 (2.25 mm) for 2 larger sizes: set of 5 double-pointed (dpn). Adjust needle size if necessary to obtain the correct gauge.

Notions Marker (m); cable needle (cn); tapestry needle.

Gauge 37 sts and 42 rnds = 4" (10 cm) in leg patt for smallest size; 36 sts and 40 rnds = 4" (10 cm) in leg patt for 2 larger sizes.

CUFF

CO 78 sts. Arrange sts evenly onto 3 dpn, place marker (pm), and join for working in the rnd, being careful not to twist sts.

Work Cuff chart for 12 rnds.

LEG

Work Rows 1–28 of Leg chart 2 times.

HEEL

NEXT RND NEEDLE 1 Work 20 sts of Row 1 of Leg chart, sl next 6 sts to Needle 2; **NEEDLE 2** Work Row 1 of Instep chart, work 7 sts from Needle 3 onto Needle 2 according to Instep chart; place first 20 sts of rnd and last 19 sts of rnd onto one needle for heel and work Heel Dec chart across these 39 sts—71 sts rem.

Heel will be worked back and forth in rows on 32 sts rem from Heel Dec chart; rem 39 sts will be worked later for instep.

HEEL FLAP

Beg with a WS row, work in St st for 33 rows.

TURN HEEL

Work short-rows (see Glossary) as foll:

SHORT-ROW 1 (RS) K17, ssk, k1, turn.

SHORT-ROW 2 Sl 1, p3, p2tog, p1, turn.

SHORT-ROW 3 Sl 1, knit to 1 st before gap created on previous row, ssk, k1, turn.

SHORT-ROW 4 Sl 1, purl to 1 st before gap created on previous row, p2tog, p1, turn.

Rep Short-rows 3 and 4 five more times—18 heel sts rem.

SHAPE GUSSET

NEXT RND With an empty needle (Needle 1), knit 18 heel sts, pick up and knit 16 sts along edge of heel flap; work Row 2 of Instep chart (Needles 2 and 3); with another needle (Needle 4), pick up and knit 16 sts along edge of heel flap, k9 from Needle 1—89 sts total; 25 sts each on Needles 1 and 4, 19 sts on Needle 2, 20 sts on Needle 3.

NEXT RND NEEDLE 1 Knit; **NEEDLES 2 AND 3** Work next row of Instep chart; **NEEDLE 4** Knit.

Rep last row 2 more times.

NEXT RND (dec rnd) **NEEDLE 1** Knit to last 3 sts, k2tog, k1; **NEEDLES 2 AND 3** Work next row of Instep chart; **NEEDLE 4** K1, ssk, knit to end—2 sts dec'd.

Rep last 3 rnds 8 more times, ending with Row 2 of Instep chart—71 sts rem; 16 sts each on Needles 1 and 4, 19 sts on Needle 2, 20 sts on Needle 3.

FOOT

Work even in patt until foot measures 7¼ (7½, 8)" (18.5 [19, 20.5] cm) from back of heel.

TOE

NEXT RND (dec rnd) **NEEDLE 1** Knit; **NEEDLES 2 AND 3** Work next row of Instep chart and at the same time dec 3 sts on Needle 2 and 4 sts on Needle 3; **NEEDLE 4** Knit—64 sts rem.

NEXT RND (dec rnd) **NEEDLES 1 AND 3** Knit to last 3 sts, k2tog, k1; **NEEDLES 2 AND 4** K1, ssk, knit to end—4 sts dec'd.

Rep last rnd every 4th rnd once more, every 3rd rnd 2 times, every 2nd rnd 3 times, then every rnd 3 times—24 sts rem.

NEXT RND NEEDLES 1 AND 3 Knit to last 2 sts, k2tog; **NEEDLES 2 AND 4** Ssk, knit to end—20 sts rem.

FINISHING

Knit sts on Needle 1. Sl sts from Needle 4 onto Needle 1 and from Needle 3 onto Needle 2. Cut yarn, leaving a 24" (61 cm) tail. With tail threaded on a tapestry needle, use Kitchener st (see Glossary) to graft rem sts tog. Weave in loose ends.

CUFF

1

HEEL DECREASE

1

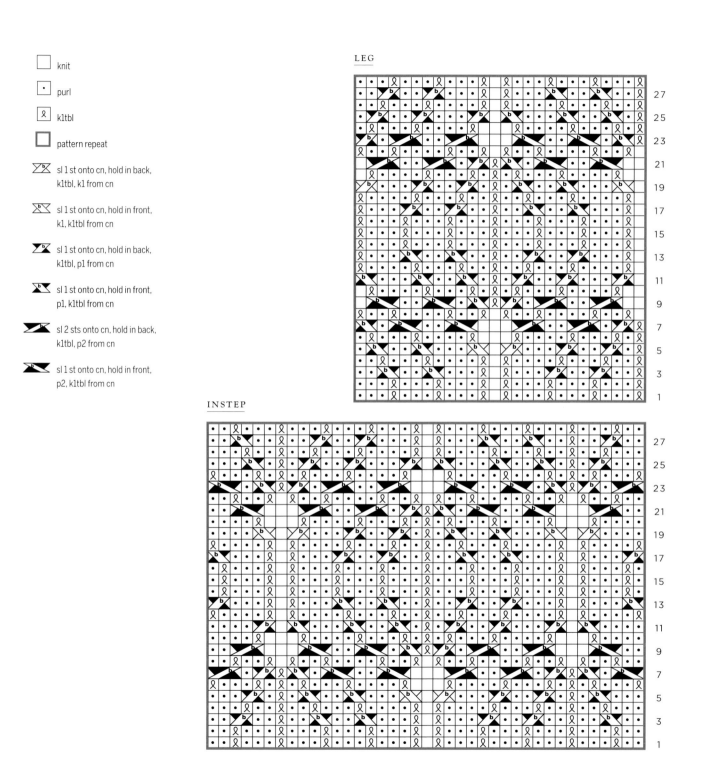

knit

· purl

Ջ k1tbl

pattern repeat

sl 1 st onto cn, hold in back,
k1tbl, k1 from cn

sl 1 st onto cn, hold in front,
k1, k1tbl from cn

sl 1 st onto cn, hold in back,
k1tbl, p1 from cn

sl 1 st onto cn, hold in front,
p1, k1tbl from cn

sl 2 sts onto cn, hold in back,
k1tbl, p2 from cn

sl 1 st onto cn, hold in front,
p2, k1tbl from cn

LEG

INSTEP

SCENT OF LAVENDER

FRANCE

A variety of lace patterns originated in Spain, but lace knitted socks came into their own in France. These created quite a sensation, especially in England, where Henry VIII owned many pairs of French-made lace stockings.

Finished size 8 (8, 8¼)" (20.5 [20.5, 21] cm) foot circumference and 9½ (9¾, 10¼)" (24 [25, 26] cm) long from back of heel to tip of toe. To fit U.S. women's shoe sizes 5–6½ (7–8½, 9–10½) (European sizes 36–37 [38–39, 40–41]). Socks shown measure 9¾" (25 cm) long.

Yarn Fingering (Super Fine #1). *Shown here:* Regia 4-ply (75% wool, 25% nylon; 229 yd [209 m]/50 g): #1991 light charcoal, 2 balls.

Needles U.S. size 1 (2.25 mm) for 2 smaller sizes, or U.S. size 2 (2.75 mm) for largest size: set of 5 double-pointed (dpn). Adjust needle size if necessary to obtain the correct gauge.

Notions Marker (m); tapestry needle.

Gauge 34 sts and 40 rnds = 4" (10 cm) in lace patt, slightly stretched, for 2 smaller sizes; 32 sts and 40 rnds = 4" (10 cm) in lace patt, slightly stretched, for largest size.

CUFF

CO 64 sts. Arrange sts evenly onto 4 dpn, place marker (pm), and join for working in the rnd, being careful not to twist sts.

Work in k1 through back loop (tbl), p1 rib for 16 rnds.

LEG

Work Rows 1–16 of Leg chart 2 times, then work Rows 1–8 once more. Sl first st of Needle 4 to Needle 3—16 sts each on Needles 1 and 2, 17 sts on Needle 3, 15 sts on Needle 4.

HEEL

NEXT ROW NEEDLE 1 [K1tbl, p1] 8 times, turn. Place 16 sts of Needle 1 and 15 sts of Needle 4 onto one needle—31 sts total. Heel will be worked back and forth in rows on these 31 sts; rem 33 sts will be worked later for instep.

HEEL FLAP

ROW 1 (WS) P1, [p1tbl, k1] 14 times, p1tbl, p1.

ROW 2 K1, [k1tbl, p1] 14 times, k1tbl, k1.

Rep Rows 1 and 2 fifteen more times, then work Row 1 once more.

TURN HEEL

Work short-rows (see Glossary) as foll:

SHORT-ROW 1 (RS) Work 16 sts in patt, ssk, k1, turn.

SHORT-ROW 2 Sl 1, work 2 sts in patt, p2tog, p1, turn.

SHORT-ROW 3 Sl 1, work in patt to 1 st before gap created on previous row, ssk, k1, turn.

SHORT-ROW 4 Sl 1, work in patt to 1 st before gap created on previous row, p2tog, p1, turn.

Rep Short-rows 3 and 4 five more times—17 heel sts rem.

LEG

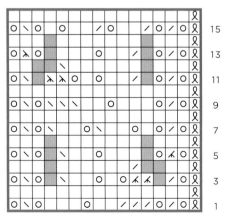

INSTEP

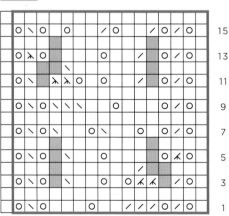

Legend:

- ☐ knit
- ☖ k1tbl
- ○ yo
- ╱ k2tog
- ╲ ssk
- ⅄ k3tog
- ⋏ sssk
- ▨ no stitch
- ☐ pattern repeat

SHAPE GUSSET

NEXT RND With an empty needle (Needle 1), k17 heel sts, pick up and knit 17 sts along edge of heel flap; work Row 9 of Instep chart (Needles 2 and 3); with another needle (Needle 4), pick up and knit 17 sts along edge of heel flap, k7 heel sts from Needle 1, k2tog from Needle 1—83 sts total; 25 sts each on Needles 1 and 4, 16 sts on Needle 2, 17 sts on Needle 3.

NEXT RND **NEEDLE 1** Knit; **NEEDLES 2 AND 3** Work next row of Instep chart; **NEEDLE 4** Knit.

Rep last rnd once more.

NEXT RND (dec rnd) **NEEDLE 1** Knit to last 3 sts, k2tog, k1; **NEEDLES 2 AND 3** Work next row of Instep chart; **NEEDLE 4** K1, ssk, knit to end—2 sts dec'd.

Rep last 3 rnds 7 more times—67 sts rem; 17 sts on Needles 1, 3, and 4; 16 sts on Needle 2.

FOOT

Work even in patt as established until foot measures about 7¼ (7½, 8)" (18.5 [19, 20.5] cm) from back of heel, ending with Row 8 or 16 of Instep chart.

TOE

NEXT RND (dec rnd) **NEEDLE 1** [P1, k1tbl] 7 times, k2tog, k1; **NEEDLE 2** K2, [p1, k1tbl] 7 times; **NEEDLE 3** [P1, k1tbl] 7 times, k2tog, k1; **NEEDLE 4** K1, ssk, [p1, k1tbl] 7 times—64 sts rem.

Work sts as they appear for 3 rnds.

NEXT RND (dec rnd) **NEEDLES 1 AND 3** Work in patt as established to last 3 sts, k2tog, k1; **NEEDLES 2 AND 4** K1, ssk, work in patt to end—4 sts dec'd.

Rep last rnd every 3rd rnd 2 more times, every 2nd rnd 3 times, then every rnd 4 times—24 sts rem.

NEXT RND (dec rnd) **NEEDLES 1 AND 3** Knit to last 2 sts, k2tog; **NEEDLES 2 AND 4** Ssk, knit to end—20 sts rem.

Knit sts on Needle 1.

FINISHING

Sl sts from Needle 4 onto Needle 1 and from Needle 3 onto Needle 2. Cut yarn, leaving a 24" (61 cm) tail. With tail threaded on a tapestry needle, use Kitchener st (see Glossary) to graft rem sts tog. Weave in loose ends.

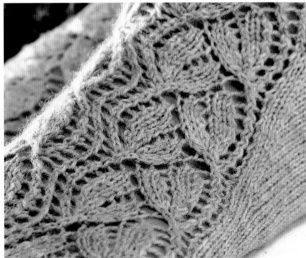

FEMININE LACE

SPAIN

Knitting in Spain shows the influences of the stranded knitting of North Africa and the Christian motifs created for liturgical purposes. It is considered by many to be the cradle of lace knitting.

Finished size 7¾ (8, 8)" (19.5 [20.5, 20.5] cm) foot circumference and 9¾ (10, 10½)" (25 [25.5, 26.5] cm) long from back of heel to tip of toe. To fit U.S. women's shoe sizes 5–6½ (7–8½, 9–10½) (European sizes 36–37 [38–39, 40–41]). Socks shown measure 10" (25.5 cm) long.

Yarn Fingering (Super Fine #1). *Shown here:* Regia 4-ply (75% wool, 25% nylon; 229 yd [209 m]/50 g): #2066 black, 2 balls. (See Notes.)

Needles U.S. size 0 (2 mm) for smallest size, or U.S. size 1 (2.25 mm) for 2 larger sizes: set of 5 double-pointed (dpn).

Adjust needle size if necessary to obtain the correct gauge.

Notions Marker (m); tapestry needle.

Gauge 42 sts and 44 rnds = 4" (10 cm) in leg patt, slightly stretched, for smallest size; 40 sts and 42 rnds = 4" (10 cm) in leg patt, slightly stretched, for 2 larger sizes.

40 sts and 44 rnds = 4" (10 cm) in instep patt for smallest size; 38 sts and 42 rnds = 4" (10 cm) in instep patt for 2 larger sizes.

Notes For U.S. women's shoe sizes 5–6½ (European sizes 36–37), use Regia 3-ply.

STITCH GUIDE

Inc 2

Insert needle into center of st 3 rows below and knit (but do not drop st from left needle); knit st on left needle (and drop st off); knit into center of same st 3 rows below—2 sts inc'd.

CUFF

CO 84 sts. Arrange sts evenly onto 3 dpn, place marker (pm), and join for working in the rnd, being careful not to twist sts.

Work 4 rnds in garter st (*knit 1 rnd, purl 1 rnd; rep from *).

Work Rows 1–3 of Cuff chart 4 times.

LEG

Work Rows 1–21 of Leg chart once, then work Rows 1–18 once more.

NEXT RND **NEEDLE 1** Work Row 19 of Leg chart, omitting inc 2 and working p1 instead; **NEEDLES 2 AND 3** Work Row 19 of Leg chart as written.

HEEL

ROW 1 (RS) **NEEDLE 1** K27, sl 1 st to Needle 2, turn.

ROW 2 (WS) K1, p39 (26 sts from Needle 1 and 13 sts from Needle 3), k1 from Needle 3—41 sts total.

Heel will be worked back and forth in rows on these 41 sts; rem 43 sts will be worked later for instep.

HEEL FLAP

ROW 1 K4, *k2tog, k6; rep from * 3 more times, k2tog, k3, turn—36 heel sts rem.

ROW 2 Purl.

ROW 3 K1, *sl 1, k1; rep from * to last st, k1.

Rep Rows 2 and 3 fifteen more times, then work Row 2 once more.

TURN HEEL

Work short-rows (see Glossary) as foll:

SHORT-ROW 1 (RS) K19, ssk, k1, turn.

SHORT-ROW 2 Sl 1, p3, p2tog, p1, turn.

SHORT-ROW 3 Sl 1, knit to 1 st before gap created on previous row, ssk, k1, turn.

SHORT-ROW 4 Sl 1, purl to 1 st before gap created on previous row, p2tog, p1, turn.

Rep Short-rows 3 and 4 six more times—20 heel sts rem.

☐ knit

· purl

ℛ k1tbl

○ yo

╱ k2tog

╲ ssk

⋏ sl 1, k2tog, psso

⊻ inc 2 (see Stitch Guide)

▨ no stitch

☐ pattern repeat

CUFF

LEG

SHAPE GUSSET

NEXT RND With an empty needle (Needle 1), k20 heel sts, pick up and knit 17 sts along edge of heel flap; work Row 1 of Instep chart (Needles 2 and 3); with another needle (Needle 4), pick up and knit 17 sts along edge of heel flap, k10 from Needle 1—97 sts total; 27 sts each on Needles 1 and 4, 22 sts on Needle 2, 21 sts on Needle 3.

Work 2 rnds in patt as established (knit sts on Needles 1 and 4; work next row of Instep chart on Needles 2 and 3).

NEXT RND (dec rnd) **NEEDLE 1** Knit to last 3 sts, k2tog, k1; **NEEDLES 2 AND 3** Work next row of Instep chart; **NEEDLE 4** K1, ssk, knit to end—2 sts dec'd.

Rep last 3 rnds 9 more times—77 sts rem; 17 sts each on Needles 1 and 4, 22 sts on Needle 2, 21 sts on Needle 3.

FOOT

Work even in patt as established until foot measures 7¼ (7½, 8)" (18.5 [19, 20.5] cm) from back of heel.

TOE

NEXT RND **NEEDLE 1** Knit; **NEEDLE 2** K1, sl last st worked to Needle 1, knit to end; **NEEDLE 3** Knit to last st, sl last st to Needle 4; **NEEDLE 4** Knit to end—18 sts each on Needles 1 and 4, 21 sts on Needle 2, 20 sts on Needle 3.

NEXT RND (dec rnd) **NEEDLE 1** K3, k2tog, k7, k2tog, k4; **NEEDLE 2** *K2tog, k2; rep from * 4 more times, k1; **NEEDLE 3** *K3, k2tog; rep from * 3 more times; **NEEDLE 4** K3, k2tog, k7, k2tog, k4—64 sts rem.

NEXT RND (dec rnd) **NEEDLES 1 AND 3** Knit to last 3 sts, k2tog, k1; **NEEDLES 2 AND 4** K1, ssk, knit to end—4 sts dec'd.

Rep dec rnd every 4th rnd once more, every 3rd rnd 3 times, every 2nd rnd 4 times, then every rnd 5 times—8 sts rem.

FINISHING

Knit sts of Needle 1. Sl sts from Needle 4 onto Needle 1 and from Needle 3 onto Needle 2. Cut yarn, leaving a 24" (61 cm) tail. With tail threaded on a tapestry needle, use Kitchener st (see Glossary) to graft rem sts tog. Weave in loose ends.

INSTEP

(chart with rows numbered 15, 13, 11, 9, 7, 5, 3, 1)

ROUTE 66

]{ mmigrants to the United States brought an enormous variety of knitting techniques from their homelands, where they disseminated them quickly. These socks are inspired by a traditional American patchwork quilt pattern called Tumbling Blocks.

Finished size 8½" (21.5 cm) circumference and 9½ (9¾, 10¼)" (24 [25, 26] cm) long from back of heel to tip of toe. To fit U.S. women's shoe sizes 5–6½ (7–8½, 9–10½) (European sizes 36–37 [38–39, 40–41]). Socks shown measure 9¾" (25 cm) long.

Yarn Fingering (Super Fine #1). *Shown here:* Regia Silk 4-ply (55% wool, 25% nylon, 20% silk; 219 yd [200 m]/ 50 g): #1237 petrol (dark blue) and #0017 light camel, 1 ball each.

Needles U.S. size 2 (2.75 mm): set of 5 double-pointed (dpn). Adjust needle size if necessary to obtain the correct gauge.

Notions Marker (m); tapestry needle.

Gauge 34 sts and 40 rnds = 4" (10 cm) in charted patt.

CUFF

With light camel, CO 64 sts. Arrange sts evenly onto 4 dpn, place marker (pm), and join for working in the rnd, being careful not to twist sts.

Work in k2, p2 rib for 12 rnds.

NEXT RND *K8, M1 (see Glossary); rep from * to end—72 sts.

LEG

Work Rows 1–14 of Patchwork chart 3 times. Break yarns.

HEEL

Sl 2 sts from Needle 2 to Needle 1 and sl 2 sts from Needle 4 to Needle 3—20 sts each on Needles 1 and 3, 16 sts each on Needles 2 and 4.

Place first 20 sts of rnd and last 16 sts of rnd onto one needle—36 sts total. Heel will be worked back and forth in rows on these 36 sts; rem 36 sts will be worked later for instep. With RS facing, join light camel.

HEEL FLAP

NEXT ROW (RS) Sl 1, *sl 1 pwise with yarn in back (wyb), k1; rep from * to last st, k1.

NEXT ROW Sl 1, purl to end.

Rep last 2 rows 16 more times.

TURN HEEL

Work short-rows (see Glossary) as foll:

SHORT-ROW 1 (RS) K19, ssk, k1, turn.

SHORT-ROW 2 Sl 1, p3, p2tog, p1, turn.

SHORT-ROW 3 Sl 1, knit to 1 st before gap

created on previous row, ssk, k1, turn.

SHORT-ROW 4 Sl 1, purl to 1 st before gap created on previous row, p2tog, p1, turn.

Rep Short-rows 3 and 4 six more times—20 heel sts rem.

SHAPE GUSSET

NEXT ROW With an empty needle (Needle 1), k20 heel sts, pick up and knit 18 sts along edge of heel flap; work Row 8 of Patchwork chart, break dark blue

(Needles 2 and 3); with another needle (Needle 4), pick up and knit 18 sts along edge of heel flap, k10 from Needle 1—92 sts total; 28 sts each on Needles 1 and 4, 18 sts each on Needles 2 and 3.

NEXT RND **NEEDLE 1** Beg as indicated for Needle 1, work Sole chart; **NEEDLES 2 AND 3** Work next row of Patchwork chart; **NEEDLE 4** Ending as indicated for Needle 4, work Sole chart.

Rep last rnd once more.

NEXT RND (dec rnd) **NEEDLE 1** Work in patt to last 2 sts, k2tog with dark blue; **NEEDLES 2 AND 3** Work next row of Patchwork chart; **NEEDLE 4** Ssk with dark blue, work in patt to end—2 sts dec'd.

Rep last 3 rnds 9 more times—72 sts rem; 18 sts on each needle.

FOOT

Work even in patt as established until foot measures 7¼ (7½, 8)" (18.5 [19, 20.5] cm) from back of heel. Break dark blue.

TOE

NEXT RND (dec rnd) **NEEDLES 1 AND 3** Knit to last 3 sts, k2tog, k1; **NEEDLES 2 AND 4** K1, ssk, knit to end—4 sts dec'd.

Rep dec rnd every 4th rnd once more, every 3rd rnd 2 times, every 2nd rnd 3 times, then every rnd 9 times—8 sts rem.

FINISHING

Break yarn, leaving an 8" (20.5 cm) tail. With tail threaded on a tapestry needle, draw through rem sts and pull tight. Fasten off on WS. Weave in loose ends.

SOLE

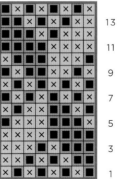

1

beg needle 1;
end needle 4

■ dark blue

× light camel

☐ pattern repeat

PATCHWORK

13
11
9
7
5
3
1

COLORS OF THE ANDES

SOUTH AMERICA

The motifs in the colorful embroidery of South America are related to the strong weaving tradition. In addition to geometric patterns such as diamonds and diagonal lines, birds and animals appear frequently.

Finished size 8½" (21.5 cm) circumference and 9½ (10, 10¼)" (24 [25.5, 26] cm) long from back of heel to tip of toe. To fit U.S. women's shoe sizes 5–6½ (7–8½, 9–10½) (European sizes 36–37 [38–39, 40–41]). Socks shown measure 10" (25.5 cm) long.

Yarn Fingering (Super Fine #1). *Shown here:* Regia 4-ply (75% wool, 25% nylon; 229 yd [209 m]/50 g):

#1229 biscuit, #1081 ruby, #1087 lagoon (light blue), and #1988 lavender (medium blue), 1 ball each.

Needles U.S. size 2 (2.75 mm): set of 5 double-pointed (dpn). Adjust needle size if necessary to obtain the correct gauge.

Notions Marker (m); tapestry needle.

Gauge 34 sts and 40 rnds = 4" (10 cm) in charted patt.

CUFF

With medium blue, CO 72 sts. Arrange sts evenly onto 4 dpn, place marker (pm), and join for working in the rnd, being careful not to twist sts.

With medium blue, work in k2, p2 rib for 1 rnd.

Work 2 rnds as foll: *k2 with medium blue, p2 with light blue; rep from * to end.

With light blue, work in k2, p2 rib for 2 rnds.

Work 2 rnds as foll: *k2 with light blue, p2 with medium blue; rep from * to end.

With medium blue, work in k2, p2 rib for 2 rnds.

Work 2 rnds as foll: *k2 with medium blue, p2 with biscuit; rep from * to end.

With biscuit, work in k2, p2 rib for 2 rnds.

FOOT

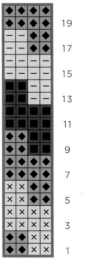

19
17
15
13
11
9
7
5
3
1

LEG

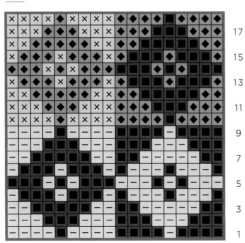

17
15
13
11
9
7
5
3
1

biscuit

ruby

light blue

medium blue

pattern repeat

LEG

Work Rows 1–18 of Leg chart once, then work Rows 1–9 once more.

HEEL

With medium blue, knit to end of Needle 1. Place first 18 sts of rnd and last 18 sts of rnd onto one needle, keeping beg of rnd marker in place—36 sts total. Heel is worked back and forth using short-rows (see Glossary) over these 36 sts; rem 36 sts will be worked later for instep. Work heel in medium blue; break other colors.

HEEL TOP

SHORT-ROW 1 (WS) Slyo (see Glossary), p35, turn.

SHORT-ROW 2 Slyo, knit to slyo created on previous row, turn.

SHORT-ROW 3 Slyo, purl to slyo created on previous row, turn.

Rep Short-rows 2 and 3 eleven more times, then work Short-row 2 once more but do not turn—13 slyo sts at each end of heel, 10 plain sts in center.

Work to end of rnd in St st, being careful to work each slyo as 1 st. Work 1 more rnd even.

HEEL BOTTOM

Work back and forth on 36 sts of heel as foll:

SHORT-ROW 1 (RS) Knit to last 12 heel sts, turn.

SHORT-ROW 2 Slyo, p11, turn.

SHORT-ROW 3 Slyo, knit to slyo created on previous row, knit slyo as 1 st, k1, turn.

SHORT-ROW 4 Slyo, purl to slyo created on previous row, purl slyo as 1 st, p1, turn.

Rep Short-rows 3 and 4 eleven more times.

NEXT ROW Slyo, k17 (to end of rnd)—first and last sts of heel are slyos.

FOOT

Resume working in the rnd, working rem 2 slyo as 1 st on first rnd. Work Foot chart until foot measures 7¼ (7¾, 8)" (18.5 [19.5, 20.5] cm) from back of heel.

TOE

Toe is worked in medium blue; break other yarns. Knit 1 rnd.

NEXT RND (dec rnd) **NEEDLES 1 AND 3** Knit to last 3 sts, k2tog, k1; **NEEDLES 2 AND 4** K1, ssk, knit to end—4 sts dec'd.

Rep dec rnd every 4th rnd once more, every 3rd rnd 2 times, every 2nd rnd 3 times, then every rnd 9 times—8 sts rem.

FINISHING

Break yarn, leaving an 8" (20.5 cm) tail. With tail threaded on a tapestry needle, draw through rem sts and pull tight. Fasten off on WS.

EMBROIDERY

Cut 3 strands of biscuit and 2 strands of ruby, each about 19¾" (50 cm) long. With biscuit threaded on a tapestry needle, use a running st to pass over 2 sts and under 2 sts on every Row 8 of Foot chart as shown. Rep with ruby on every Row 20. Weave in loose ends.

RIOT OF COLOR

MOROCCO

The colorfully patterned motifs of North Africa are exciting and luminous. The traditional tiles are abundantly embellished and decorated with gold accents and artful ornaments. Saturated tones of red from crimson to ruby are often on display.

Finished size 8¾" (22 cm) foot circumference and 9½ (10¼, 11)" (24 [26, 28] cm) long from back of heel to tip of toe. To fit U.S. women's shoe sizes 5–6½ (7–8½, 9–10½) (European sizes 36–37 [38–39, 40–41]). Socks shown measure 10¼" (26 cm) long.

Yarn Fingering (Super Fine #1). *Shown here:* Regia 4-ply (75% wool, 25% nylon; 229 yd [209 m]/50 g): #1078 cardinal, 2 balls, and #2002 cherry, 1 ball.

Needles U.S. size 1 (2.25 mm): set of 5 double-pointed (dpn). Adjust needle size if necessary to obtain the correct gauge.

Notions Marker (m); about 2 yd (2 m) gold metallic embroidery thread; tapestry needle.

Gauge 36 sts and 40 rnds = 4" (10 cm) in charted patt.

STITCH GUIDE

Rotation

Bring right needle to back of work, down and under knitted fabric, then in front of fabric and up—right needle has made one rotation around knitted fabric, and 1 twist is inserted in fabric between needles.

CUFF

With cherry, CO 72 sts. Do not join. Knit 1 row. With cardinal, knit 2 rows. With cherry, knit 2 rows.

NEXT ROW With cherry, k3, *1 rotation (see Stitch Guide), k6; rep from * to last 3 sts, 1 rotation, k3. Arrange sts evenly onto 4 dpn, place marker (pm), and join for working in the rnd, being careful not to twist sts.

With cardinal, work in k1 through back loop (tbl), p1 rib for 10 rnds.

LEG

NEXT RND *K9, M1 (see Glossary); rep from * to end—80 sts.

Work Rows 1–12 of Border chart.

Work Rows 1–24 of Tile chart. Break both yarns.

HEEL

Place first 20 sts of rnd and last 20 sts of rnd onto one needle—40 sts total. Heel will be worked back and forth in rows on these 40 sts; rem 40 sts will be worked later for instep.

HEEL FLAP

With RS facing, join cardinal.

NEXT ROW (RS) Knit.

NEXT ROW (dec row) K1, p2, *p2tog, p6; rep from * 3 more times, p2tog, p2, k1—35 sts rem.

NEXT ROW Knit.

NEXT ROW K1, purl to last st, k1.

Rep last 2 rows 15 more times.

TURN HEEL

Work short-rows (see Glossary) as foll:

SHORT-ROW 1 (RS) K19, ssk, k1, turn.

SHORT-ROW 2 Sl 1, p4, p2tog, p1, turn.

SHORT-ROW 3 Sl 1, knit to 1 st before gap created on previous row, ssk, k1, turn.

SHORT-ROW 4 Sl 1, purl to 1 st before gap created on previous row, p2tog, p1, turn.

Rep Short-rows 3 and 4 five more times—21 heel sts rem.

NEXT SHORT-ROW (RS) Sl 1, knit to 1 st before gap created on previous row, ssk, turn—20 heel sts rem.

NEXT SHORT-ROW Sl 1, purl to 1 st before gap created on previous row, p2tog, turn—19 heel sts rem.

SHAPE GUSSET

NEXT RND With an empty needle (Needle 1), k19 heel sts, pick up and knit 16 sts along edge of heel flap; work Row 1 of Tile

■ cardinal

+ cherry

□ pattern repeat

TILE

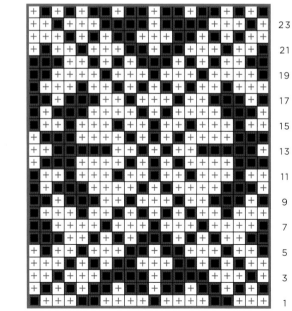

23
21
19
17
15
13
11
9
7
5
3
1

BORDER

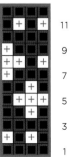

11
9
7
5
3
1

chart (Needles 2 and 3); with another needle (Needle 4), pick up and knit 16 sts along edge of heel flap, k9 from Needle 1—91 sts total; 26 sts on Needle 1, 20 sts each on Needles 2 and 3, 25 sts on Needle 4.

NEXT RND NEEDLE 1 *K1 with cherry, k1 with cardinal; rep from * to last 2 sts, k2 with cherry; **NEEDLES 2 AND 3** Work next row of Tile chart; **NEEDLE 4** K2 with cherry, *k1 with cardinal, k1 with cherry; rep from * to last st, k1 with cardinal.

Rep last rnd 2 more times.

NEXT RND (dec rnd) NEEDLE 1 Work in patt to last 3 sts, k2tog with cherry, k1 with cherry; **NEEDLES 2 AND 3** Work next row of Tile chart; **NEEDLE 4** K1 with cherry, ssk with cherry, work sts in colors as they appear to end—2 sts dec'd.

Cont in patt, rep dec rnd every 4th rnd 5 more times—79 sts rem; 20 sts each on Needles 1–3, 19 sts on Needle 4.

FOOT

Work even in patt as established for 30 (36, 43) more rnds, ending with Row 7 (13, 20) of Tile chart. With cardinal, knit 1 rnd. Break cherry.

TOE

NEXT RND (dec rnd) *K3, k2tog; rep from * 14 more times, k4—64 sts rem; 16 sts on each needle.

NEXT RND (dec rnd) NEEDLES 1 AND 3 Knit to last 3 sts, k2tog, k1; **NEEDLES 2 AND 4** K1, ssk, knit to end—4 sts dec'd.

Rep dec rnd every 4th rnd once more, every 3rd rnd 2 times, every 2nd rnd 3 times, then every rnd 7 times—8 sts rem.

FINISHING

Break yarn, leaving an 8" (20.5 cm) tail. With tail threaded on a tapestry needle, draw through rem sts and pull tight. Fasten off on WS. Weave in loose ends.

EMBROIDERY

With gold threaded on a tapestry needle, embroider stars between twists at cuff.

HERRINGBONE FROM KIEL

GERMANY

In Northern Germany, you hardly see the abundant diversity of patterns found in the alpine regions. The knitting patterns are simpler, the lines are clear and unadorned. The style is graphic, and the designs are reminiscent of weaving patterns.

Finished size 8¼" (21 cm) circumference and 9¾ (10¼, 10½)" (25 [26, 26.5] cm) long from back of heel to tip of toe. To fit U.S. women's shoe sizes 5–6½ (7–8½, 9–10½) (European sizes 36–37 [38–39, 40–41]). Socks shown measure 10¼" (26 cm) long.

Yarn Fingering (Super Fine #1). *Shown here:* Regia Cotton 4-ply (41% wool, 34% cotton, 25% nylon; 220 yd [201 m]/50 g): #0037 petrol (dark blue), 2 balls, and #0088 turquoise, 1 ball. (See Notes.)

Needles U.S. size 2 (2.75 mm): set of 5 double-pointed (dpn). Adjust needle size if necessary to obtain the correct gauge.

Notions Marker (m); tapestry needle.

Gauge 34 sts and 40 rnds = 4" (10 cm) in herringbone patt.

Notes For U.S. women's shoe sizes 5–6½ (European sizes 36–37), choose 100% wool yarn.

CUFF

With dark blue, CO 60 sts. Arrange sts evenly onto 4 dpn, place marker (pm), and join for working in the rnd, being careful not to twist sts.

Work in k1, p1 rib for 15 rnds.

NEXT RND *K6, M1 (see Glossary); rep from * to end—70 sts; 17 sts each on Needles 1 and 3, 18 sts each on Needles 2 and 4.

LEG

Work Rows 1–4 of Herringbone chart 10 times, then work Rows 1 and 2 once more; piece measures about 6¼" (16 cm) from CO. Sl last 2 sts of Needle 1 onto Needle 2 and last 2 sts of Needle 3 onto Needle 4—15 sts each on Needles 1 and 3, 20 sts each on Needles 2 and 4.

HEEL

Heel is worked back and forth using short-rows (see Glossary) over 35 sts of Needles 1 and 4; rem 35 sts will be worked later for instep. Work heel in dark blue; break turquoise.

HEEL TOP

SHORT-ROW 1 (RS) K15, turn.

SHORT-ROW 2 Slyo (see Glossary), purl to end, turn.

SHORT-ROW 3 Slyo, knit to slyo created on previous row, turn.

SHORT-ROW 4 Slyo, purl to slyo created on previous row, turn.

Rep Short-rows 3 and 4 ten more times, then work Short-row 3 once more, but do not turn—12 slyo sts at each end of heel, 11 plain sts in center.

NEXT RND NEEDLE 1 Knit, being careful to work slyo as 1 st; **NEEDLES 2 AND 3** Attach turquoise, work next row of Herringbone chart, break turquoise; **NEEDLE 4** Knit, being careful to work slyo as 1 st. Work 1 more rnd even.

HEEL BOTTOM

Work back and forth on 35 sts of Needles 1 and 4 as foll:

SHORT-ROW 1 (RS) Knit to last 11 sts of Needle 1, turn.

SHORT-ROW 2 Slyo, p12, turn.

SHORT-ROW 3 Slyo, knit to slyo created on previous row, knit slyo as 1 st, k1, turn.

SHORT-ROW 4 Slyo, purl to slyo created on previous row, purl slyo as 1 st, p1, turn.

Rep Short-rows 3 and 4 ten more times.

NEXT ROW Slyo, k19 (to end of rnd)—first and last sts of heel are slyos.

HERRINGBONE

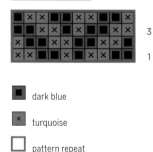

3

1

■ dark blue

✕ turquoise

☐ pattern repeat

FOOT

Resume working in the rnd, working rem 2 slyo as 1 st on first rnd. Rep Rows 1–4 of Herringbone chart until foot measures 7¼ (7¾, 8)" (18.5 [19.5, 20.5] cm) from back of heel, ending with Row 2 or 4 of chart. Break turquoise.

NEXT RND (dec rnd) **NEEDLE 1** K15; **NEEDLE 2** K16, k2tog, sl next 2 sts to Needle 3; **NEEDLE 3** K17; **NEEDLE 4** K16, k2tog, sl next 2 sts to Needle 1—68 sts rem; 17 sts on each needle.

TOE

NEXT RND (dec rnd) **NEEDLES 1 AND 3** Knit to last 3 sts, k2tog, k1; **NEEDLES 2 AND 4** K1, ssk, knit to end—4 sts dec'd.

Rep dec rnd every 4th rnd once more, every 3rd rnd 2 times, every 2nd rnd 3 times, then every rnd 8 times—8 sts rem.

FINISHING

Break yarn, leaving an 8" (20.5 cm) tail. With tail threaded on a tapestry needle, draw through rem sts and pull tight. Fasten off on WS. Weave in loose ends.

GLOSSARY & KNITTING TECHNIQUES

ABBREVIATIONS

beg(s) begin(s); beginning
BO bind off
CC contrasting color
cm centimeter(s)
cn cable needle
CO cast on
cont continue(s); continuing
dec(s) decrease(s); decreasing
dpn double-pointed needles
foll follow(s); following
g gram(s)
inc(s) increase(s); increasing
k knit
k1f&b knit into the front and back of same stitch
kwise knitwise, as if to knit
m marker(s)
MC main color
mm millimeter(s)
M1 make one (increase)
M1L make one left (increase)
M1p make one purlwise (increase)
M1R make one right (increase)
p purl
p1f&b purl into front and back of same stitch
patt(s) pattern(s)
psso pass slipped stitch over
pwise purlwise, as if to purl
rem remain(s); remaining
rep repeat(s); repeating
rev St st reverse stockinette stitch
rnd(s) round(s)
RS right side
sl slip
sl st slip st (slip 1 stitch purlwise unless otherwise indicated)

ssk slip 2 stitches knitwise, one at a time, from the left needle to right needle, insert left needle tip through both front loops
and knit together from this position (1 stitch decrease)
st(s) stitch(es)
St st stockinette stitch
tbl through back loop
tog together
WS wrong side

wyb with yarn in back
wyf with yarn in front
yd yard(s)
yo yarnover
* repeat starting point
** repeat all instructions between asterisks
( ) alternate measurements and/or instructions
[ ] work instructions as a group a specified number of times

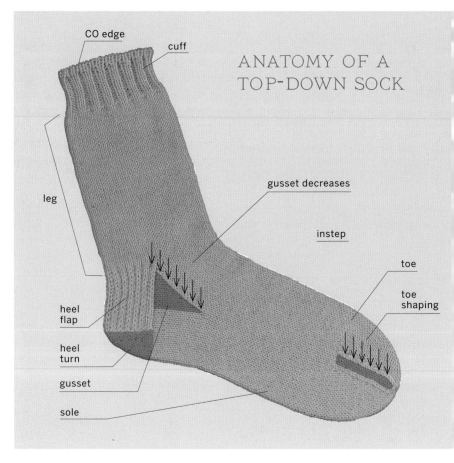

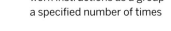
ANATOMY OF A
TOP-DOWN SOCK

CO edge
cuff
leg
heel flap
heel turn
gusset
sole
gusset decreases
instep
toe
toe shaping

STITCH DISTRIBUTION & NUMBERING OF NEEDLES

The instructions in each pattern give the number of stitches on each needle.

WORKING ON FOUR NEEDLES From the CO edge, stitches are divided among needles that are numbered clockwise, usually beginning at the back of the heel (**FIGURE 1**). The heel is generally worked on the stitches on Needles 1 and 4, so that the beginning of the round is at the back of the sock and under the foot. However, for some patterns it is simpler to have the beginning of the round at the side of the sock and work the heel on a different pair of needles.

WORKING ON THREE NEEDLES Sometimes it is simpler to divide the stitches among three needles (**FIGURE 2**). In this case, the heel is usually worked on half of the stitches. Stitches are then redistributed before knitting the heel by slipping stitches from one needle to another.

WORKING ON TWO CIRCULAR NEEDLES When working large pattern repeats, it is sometimes easier to use two circular needles instead of four double points. Stitches are then divided such that one needle holds the stitches for the front of the leg and the other needle holds the stitches for the back of the leg (**FIGURE 3**). The sole and instep stitches are divided in the same way.

To set up for working on two circular needles, cast all stitches onto one circular needle, then slip one-half of the stitches onto the cable of a second circular needle, or cast the appropriate number of stitches directly onto each needle. Join for working in the round, being careful not to twist the cast-on. When using this method, it is very important to keep the needles from getting mixed up. Knit the first half of the stitches from one end to the other of the first needle (the needle on which they sit) while the second needle "rests," then do the same with the other stitches and needle.

The heel is centered on the beginning of the round as for other methods. In the round before beginning the heel, rearrange the stitches to center the heel as foll: Work all stitches of Needle 1 as established, then work the stitches that would be on Dpn 3 from Needle 2 to Needle 1. With Needle 2, work the remaining stitches from Needle 2, then work the stitches that would be on Dpn 1 from Needle 1 to Needle 2. This rotates the sock one-quarter round.

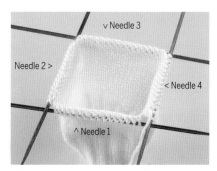

Figure 1: Working on four needles

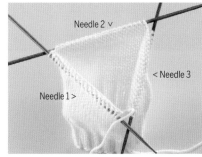

Figure 2: Working on three needles

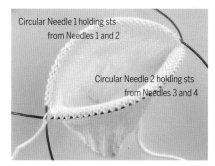

Figure 3: Working on circular needles

SHORT-ROW HEELS

SLIPPED YARNOVER (SLYO) Slipped yarnovers make it possible to knit a short-row heel with no holes.

After turning the work, bring the yarn to the front as if to purl. With the right needle, slip the next stitch as if to purl **(FIGURE 1)**. Wrap the yarn over the top of the right-hand needle and pull tightly so that both legs of the stitch from the row below are stretched over the needle **(FIGURE 2)**. Bring the working yarn to the back of the right needle before working the next stitch.

Slipped yarnovers are worked the same way on both right side and wrong side rows. To continue purling a WS row, bring the yarn to the front under the right needle **(FIGURE 3)**.

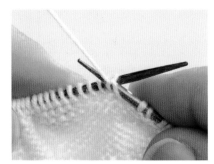

Figure 1: Slip one stitch purlwise

Figure 2: Pull yarn tightly over needle

Figure 3: Bring yarn to front under right needle

WORKING A SLIPPED YARNOVER To knit a slipped yarn-over, carefully insert the right needle under both legs of the stitch and work them together (shown from the right side in **FIGURE 1** and from the wrong side in **FIGURE 2**). Be careful not to mistake each leg of the stitch for two separate stitches and accidentally increase.

Figure 1: Working a slipped yarnover

Figure 2: Working a slipped yarnover

RIGHT- & LEFT-LEANING DECREASES

The way that two stitches are knitted together determines whether they lean to the right or to the left. These decreases are important when knitting lace patterns, uniform gusset decreases on a heel, or symmetrical toe shaping.

RIGHT-LEANING DECREASE (K2TOG) Insert right-hand needle into two stitches at once and knit them together **(FIGURE 1)**.

LEFT-LEANING DECREASE (SSK) Slip two stitches, one at a time, from left needle to right needle **(FIGURE 2)**. Insert left needle tip through both front loops and knit stitches together **(FIGURE 3)**.

Figure 1: Right-leaning decrease (k2tog)

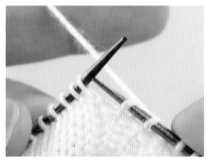

Figure 2: Left-leaning decrease (ssk), Step 1

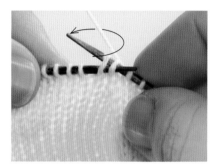

Figure 3: Left-leaning decrease (ssk), Step 2

TWISTED TRAVELING STITCHES

Many patterns from Alpine countries owe their beauty to twisted traveling stitches.

TWISTED KNIT Work a twisted knit stitch (k1tbl) by inserting the right needle into the back of the next stitch from right to left, then wrapping the yarn to knit it as usual **(FIGURE 1)**. The stitch has been rotated 180° and appears more pronounced.

TWISTED PURL Work a twisted purl stitch (p1tbl) by inserting the right needle into the back of the stitch from left to right and proceeding to purl **(FIGURE 2)**. The stitch now appears as a twisted knit stitch on the wrong side. This technique is useful when a pattern requires twisted stitches in a heel flap, which is worked back and forth rather than in the round.

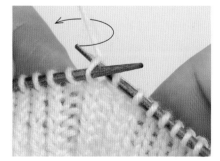

Figure 1: Twisted knit (k1tbl)

Figure 2: Twisted purl (p1tbl)

TWISTED TRAVELING STITCHES (CONT.)

RIGHT TWIST WITH CABLE NEEDLE Slip one stitch onto a cable needle and hold in back of work, knit one stitch from the left needle through the back loop, then either knit one stitch through back loop or purl one stitch from the cable needle (as given in directions).

RIGHT TWIST WITHOUT CABLE NEEDLE Insert the right needle from front to back into the right leg of the second stitch from the tip of the left needle and knit it without dropping it from the left needle **(FIGURE 1)**. Then work the first stitch as either a twisted knit stitch or a purl stitch (as given in directions) and slip both stitches off the needle.

LEFT TWIST WITH CABLE NEEDLE Slip one stitch onto a cable needle and hold in front of work, knit one stitch from the left needle through back loop, then knit one stitch from cable needle through the back loop.

LEFT TWIST WITHOUT CABLE NEEDLE Insert the right needle from right to left behind the left needle into the back leg of the second stitch on the left needle and knit it without dropping it from the left needle **(FIGURE 2)**. Then knit the first stitch through the back loop and slip both stitches off.

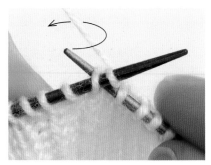
Figure 1: Right twist without a cable needle

Figure 2: Left twist without a cable needle

Figure 3: Left purl twist without a cable needle

LEFT PURL TWIST WITH CABLE NEEDLE Slip one stitch onto a cable needle and hold in front of work, purl one stitch, then knit the stitch from cable needle through the back loop.

LEFT PURL TWIST WITHOUT CABLE NEEDLE Slip the first stitch purlwise, slip the second stitch knitwise, then replace the rotated stitches on the left needle. On the WS of the work, purl the second stitch **(FIGURE 3),** but do not slip stitch from needle yet. Then knit the first stitch through back loop and slip both stitches off together.

TWO-COLOR STRANDED KNITTING

These patterns are worked with at least two colors per row, a background color and a contrast color. As a rule they are knit in stockinette stitch and indicated with charts.

While knitting with one color, the other is floating across the back of the work; the more stitches there are to be knit in a given color, the longer the floats. The floats shouldn't exceed eight to ten stitches when working with 4-ply sock yarn in U.S. needle size of 1–3 (2.25–3.25 mm).

TRAPPING THE FLOATS There is a risk of getting snagged when putting on or taking off a garment with floats. To prevent snags, catch the float about midway through its length so that it is snug against the fabric **(FIGURE 1)**. When trapping the float, prevent its showing through by trapping the yarn behind a stitch of a less contrasting color.

LENGTH OF FLOATS For a consistent fabric, it is important that the length of the floats be as even as possible. To prevent a float that is too short and causes the fabric to pucker **(FIGURE 2)**, spread out the stitches on the right needle **(FIGURE 3)**. Press your right index finger on the working yarn so that the float will be the right length.

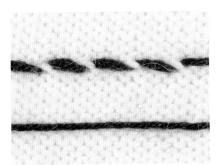

Figure 1: Trapping floats

Figure 2: Too-short floats

Figure 3: Spread out stitches on right needle

CHANGING NEEDLES The next big challenge is at the junction between two needles **(FIGURE 1)**. The most helpful technique is to spread the stitches on the needle as wide as they will be when the sock is worn and hold the yarn near the needle. After knitting the first stitch in a new color, line up the previous and new needles and measure the amount of yarn required **(FIGURE 2)**.

Beginners often find stranded knitting easier on two circular needles because the needle only changes twice per round instead of three or four times, and the flexible cable of the circular needle might make it easier to spot floats that are too tight.

Figure 1: Changing Needles

Figure 2: Changing Needles

HOLDING THE YARN How you hold your yarn is a matter of personal preference. Being relaxed and creating a smooth fabric are more important than speed. The best thing to do is to experiment with the suggested methods and figure out what works best for you.

BOTH YARNS IN THE LEFT HAND To hold both yarns in the left hand, lay them both over the left index finger **(FIGURE 1)**. You may choose to wrap them around your pinkie finger for tension. When one color is used more often than the other, it quickly becomes tight around your finger. This method of holding the yarn allows you to quickly adjust the length of both strands and return to your customary hold while knitting. One disadvan-

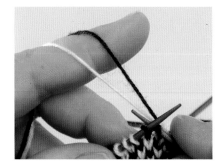

Figure 1: Both yarns in left hand

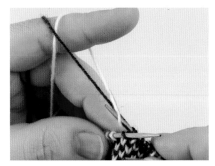

Figure 2: Variation on both yarns in left hand

tage of this method for holding yarn is that both strands are held to the same side as the working needle and can become easily twisted when adjusting the tension.

VARIATION ON BOTH YARNS IN LEFT HAND Lay the first strand as usual from back to front over the left index finger, then lay the second strand from front to back **(FIGURE 2, PREVIOUS PAGE)**. Wrap both strands together one more time around the left pinkie. This grasp prevents the twisting of the yarn, but it is more difficult to keep both strands the same length.

ONE YARN IN EACH HAND In two-handed knitting, one strand of yarn lies over each index finger **(FIGURE 3)**. Each strand must be allowed to run through the fingers at a different rate to maintain the same length. Yarns hardly ever get tangled using this method, and it is no problem to use the yarns at different rates. This grasp requires a little practice and is suitable for more experienced knitters.

ONE YARN AT A TIME The easiest way of knitting with two colors is to lay the working strand over the left index finger for Continental knitters **(FIGURE 4)** or over the right for English-style knitters. The unused strand hangs off the back of the knitting. To change colors, drop the first strand and lay the second strand over the index finger. The tension of the yarn is easiest to manage with this method, and even beginners can easily manage two yarns. It is very easy to trap a float, and as you are manually wrapping the yarns around one another, it is easy to anticipate and avoid tangles.

Figure 3: One yarn in each hand

Figure 4: One yarn at a time

GAUGE Stranded knitting fabric is always tighter than stockinette fabric, which means that more stitches are needed to work the same diameter. Stranded knitting is also less elastic, so there should be a little extra width built into the sock as well. The floats running through the inside of the sock help make it thicker and warmer than a solid color sock knit from the same yarn.

Be sure to block stranded knitting when it is complete or at least dampen and stretch gently into desired shape. It will become more even in appearance.

KNITTING WITH BEADS

Size 8° (2.6 mm) seed beads are especially well-suited for knitting socks with 4-ply yarn. Craft and bead shops offer them in many different colors and finishes.

STRINGING BEADS Before knitting the beaded patterns in the book, you will need to string the beads onto the working yarn. It is simplest to use a sewing needle. Cut a 12"–16" (30.5–40.5 cm) piece of strong sewing thread, fold it in half, and thread it through the sewing needle. Pull about 8" (20.5 cm) of yarn through the loop. With the help of the sewing needle, all the beads can be slid onto the sock yarn **(FIGURE 1)**. To count the beads, it is helpful to pick up five at a time and slide them up the yarn in blocks of fifty. Once all the beads are threaded, slide them about 3 yd farther up the yarn. Cast on the number of stitches specified and follow the instructions as usual. Slide the beads up the working thread as needed or farther down the yarn to keep them out of the way.

PLACING BEADS Where a bead stitch is indicated on the chart, insert the right needle as if to knit and slide a bead up close to the needle. As you knit the stitch, pull the bead through, too. The bead should sit on the right leg of the stitch **(FIGURE 2)**.

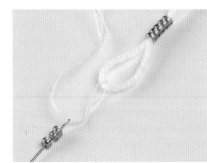

Figure 1: Stringing beads

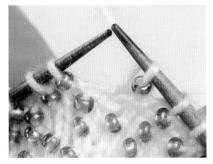

Figure 2: Bead on right leg of stitch

KNITTING TWISTED BEAD STITCHES The simplest way to place beads in knitting is with a twisted stitch. The stitch that contains a bead is worked as a twisted stitch on the next row or round, securing the bead in place. This rotates both legs of the stitch so that the beads cannot slip **(FIGURE 3)**. Be careful that the bead sits on the right leg of the stitch. This technique is most common when there is a single row of beads in the design.

Figure 3: Bead stitches in stockinette stitch

BEAD STITCHES IN STOCKINETTE STITCH Stitches are more even when beads are worked in stockinette stitches, though you have to watch closely because a bead can easily slip from the right to left leg of a stitch, changing the appearance of the pattern. Knitting beads in stockinette-stitch fabric is well-suited for knitting an entire pattern, not just one row. For this technique, work every stitch as a knit stitch regardless of whether you'll be knitting another bead.

If the bead is not placed on the right leg of the stitch, slip the beaded stitch as if to knit, then insert the left needle from left to right and knit. This allows you to control the position of the bead more easily.

Bead knitting in stockinette stitch should not be too loose. If it is, you may find that after washing, the beads have migrated to the inside of your sock.

PROVISIONAL CAST-ON

The cast-on edge of a piece of knitting that has been worked provisionally can be opened up and worked in the opposite direction. This technique can be used to add an afterthought heel, create a hem, or work a sock from side to side.

Choose a contrasting colored yarn that is somewhat thicker than the sock yarn. With a crochet hook, make a very loose chain of ten to fifteen more stitches than the desired number of knit stitches. Using the sock yarn, pick up and knit one stitch per "bump" on the back of the chain until you have the desired number of stitches **(FIGURE 1)**. Be careful not to split the strand of yarn.

When you are ready to work the cast-on stitches, loosen the end of the chain and pull out the crochet chain slowly and carefully **(FIGURE 2).** Pick up each revealed stitch and place it on a needle.

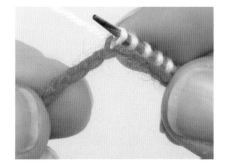

Figure 1: Provisional cast-on

Figure 2: Remove the crochet chain

KITCHENER STITCH

The Kitchener stitch can be used to attach parallel rows of live stitches to one another. Begin with the stitches to be joined on two double-pointed needles held parallel to one another with the stitches to be joined across from one another. There must be the same number of stitches on both needles. Thread a length of matching yarn on a tapestry needle; you will be mimicking the path of a new row of stitches with it.

STEP 1: Insert the tapestry needle purlwise into the first stitch on the front needle and pull the yarn through, leaving the stitch on the needle **(FIGURE 1)**.

STEP 2: Insert the tapestry needle knitwise into the first stitch on the back needle and pull the yarn through, leaving the stitch on the needle **(FIGURE 2)**.

STEP 3: Insert the tapestry needle knitwise into the next stitch on the front needle and pull the yarn through, dropping the stitch from the needle.

STEP 4: Insert the tapestry needle purlwise into the next stitch on the front needle and pull the yarn through, leaving the stitch on the needle **(FIGURE 3)**.

STEP 5: Insert the tapestry needle purlwise into the next stitch on the back needle and pull the yarn through, dropping the stitch from the needle.

STEP 6: Insert the tapestry needle knitwise into the next stitch on the back needle and pull the yarn through, leaving the stitch on the needle **(FIGURE 4)**.

Repeat Steps 3–6 to the last two stitches, then repeat Steps 3 and 5 for the remaining two stitches.

Figure 1: Step 1

Figure 2: Step 2

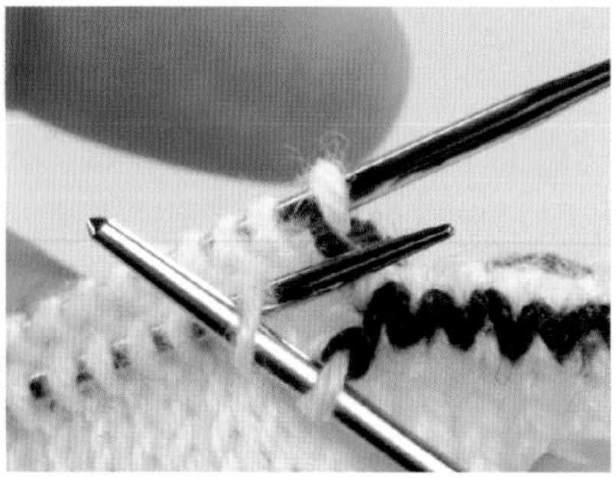

Figure 3: Steps 3 and 4

Figure 4: Steps 5 and 6

DECORATION & FINISHING TOUCHES

WEAVING IN ENDS Weaving in the ends on socks requires more care because there are no edge stitches or seams at your disposal to anchor yarn. It is fairly easy to hide ends in the cast on-edge or toe but be careful with ends in the middle of your sock, as with stranded knitting in general.

Use a sharp embroidery needle to pull ends through a single strand on the inside of the sock **(FIGURE 1)**. Floats in stranded knitting are also good places to weave in ends.

SASHIKO EMBROIDERY Cut a strip of foot-shaped cardboard to slip into the sock; this will prevent you from stitching through both layers of fabric. The sock should be stretched slightly while you work so that the embroidery doesn't pull tight when you put on the sock. Trace two copies of the sashiko design onto tissue paper and pin one to each sock. Stitch directly through the tissue on top of the lines with small stitches, placing the needle into the fabric as accurately as possible **(FIGURE 2)**. Tear out the tissue.

BALTIC BRAID Bring both strands to the front of your work. In the rounds to follow, bring the next color to be knitted to the back of the work, knit the stitch, and bring it to front again.

RND 1 *K1 in color A, k1 in color B; rep from * and *at the same time*, working in St st, lay the strand of the next color *over* the previously used strand **(FIGURE 3)**.

RND 2 * K1 in color A, k1 in color B; rep from * and *at the same time,* working in St st, bring the strand of the next color *under* the previously used strand **(FIGURE 4).**

Rep Rnds 1 and 2 as desired.

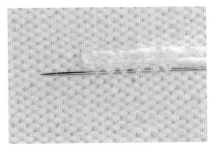

Figure 1: Weaving in ends

Figure 2: Sashiko Embroidery

Figure 3: Rnd 1 of Baltic Braid

Figure 4: Rnd 2 of Baltic Braid

ACKNOWLEDGMENTS

Many heartfelt thanks to Melitta Carola, Barbara, and Miriam, whose needles worked so diligently; to Giovanna Lo Presti for the many long discussions about color and photos; and my family, who endured the mountain of wool with me!

Thanks to Coats LLC for their support of this book.

YARN SUPPLIER

Regia
Distributed in the United States
by Westminster Fibers
165 Ledge St.
Nashua, NH 03060
westminsterfibers.com

INDEX

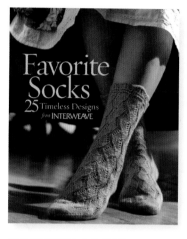